D0638770

THE FAITH OF
A CHRISTIAN

CUM OMNIBUS ILLIS
PRAECEPTORIBUS SCRIPTORIBUS AMICIS
TUM INTER EOS PRAECIFUE
PATRI MEO
QUI AD FIDEM PUERI FIRMANDAM
DEI CONSILIA APERUERUNT
HUNC LIBRUM DEDICO GRATUS

THE FAITH OF A CHRISTIAN

An Outline of Christian Belief

By

H. MARTYN CUNDY
M.A., Ph.D.

INTER-VARSITY PRESS
1519 NORTH ASTOR, CHICAGO 10, ILLINOIS

First Published	.	.	.	November 1945
Second Edition (revised and enlarged)		.	July 1947
Reprinted	.	.	.	February 1950
Reprinted	.	.	.	November 1953
Reprinted	.	.	.	. March 1955
Reprinted	.	.	.	December 1956

Made and printed in England by
STAPLES PRINTERS LIMITED
at their Rochester, Kent, establishment

CONTENTS

PREFACE

THERE are many causes which contribute to the difficulties of one who is trying for the first time to examine and appropriate the Christian revelation. He hears a bewildering variety of voices, and is confronted with an even more bewildering array of books. Many of these are theological works which he finds difficult to read, both their subject-matter and their language being unfamiliar to him. Others are more popular in style, but expound a few important doctrines only, and do not present him with an ordered system of belief. Some explanation is therefore necessary for the addition of yet another to their number.

It has been the writer's privilege to hear, and to try to answer, the questions of a number of young Christians. Many of their difficulties revealed in this way seem to him to arise from a single basic trouble: the inquirers have a fair knowledge of one or two matters directly related to their experience, but they have no logical framework into which to fit them. In short, they need a theology, a "science of God". The thoughts and lives of all great Christians have taken shape within the bounds of such a framework. We need to serve God not only with the spirit, but with the understanding also, which entails first submitting our thoughts to Christ's authority, and then ordering them into a consistent whole.

This little book tries to set out in simple language such an ordered scheme of thought and belief about God. It makes no claim to originality, and the writer must ask forgiveness if any half-remembered quotations have escaped acknowledg-

7

ment. The order adopted is intended to be a logical one, and necessary terms which may be unfamiliar are explained when first introduced. Like hurried travellers, we have paid only casual visits to the chief scenes of interest, but it is the author's hope and prayer that the reader may find that the land he passes through is a good land, and may be encouraged to explore in the company of more thorough writers the detailed topography of the kingdom of God.

SHERBORNE. *January 1945.*

PREFACE TO SECOND EDITION

THE call for a reprint of this little book provides an opportunity of making a few changes in accordance with the kind suggestions and criticisms of friends. Since also the necessity for stringent economy of space has passed, I have been able to deal a little more fully with a few matters that were rather hastily passed over before. Notable among these are the subjects of the Holy Trinity, the marks of the Church, and the interpretation of prophecy.

It has been gratifying to learn of the usefulness of the book, and this new edition is sent out, like its predecessor, in prayer that God may see fit to use it to His honour and glory.

SHERBORNE. *July, 1947.*

GOD'S REVELATION OF HIMSELF

CHAPTER I

GOD MAKES THE WORLD

THERE is a story told of a diffident preacher who asked his tutor's advice about beginning his sermons. The reply came: "Begin at the beginning, say what you have to say, and then stop!" Much the same problem confronts us when we try to put into order what Christians believe. And the answer is the same—we must begin at the beginning. The Bible makes a most uncompromising opening to its first book—Genesis, the Book of Beginnings. It reads: "In the beginning God created the heaven and the earth".

It is not popular nowadays to begin here. We would perhaps prefer to start from human need, or, as a famous advertisement puts it, "in the present state of human knowledge". But Genesis begins with God, and, furthermore, with a statement about His activity which transcends human knowledge. The writer to the Hebrews (Heb. xi, 3) reminds us, indeed, that it requires faith to understand this statement. We must not be surprised at this. The Christian revelation is reasonable enough, but it does not present its case to us as a lawyer might—and keep us straining to find the flaws in its argument. Instead it challenges us with a venture of faith; and when we know Him on whom we have ventured, in whom we have believed, we shall be persuaded of the truth of His claims.

Let us begin then at the beginning, with God as Creator. It is important to the Christian that God made the universe about us and ourselves as part of it. We can perhaps see this best by looking at the various alternatives to this belief which men have put forward. They are, roughly speaking, of four kinds: Atheism, Dualism, Polytheism and Pantheism, and all in various subtle forms are popular today.

9

Atheism is a complete and consistent denial of God and the supernatural. For the thoroughgoing atheist the world is a self-contained, self-developing entity dependent neither for its inception nor for its maintenance on any outside power or will. God is not in all his thoughts. His is a philosophy of despair. The joys of life alike with its pains are transient, illusory, purposeless. Possibly they may affect the survival value of the human race, but, to the individual, life's experiences are a mere eddy in the turbulences of existence. Such an attitude is far from rare among those who call themselves "hard-headed scientists". But it is difficult to follow it through consistently. There are moments in the lives of all of us when we feel there is more in the glory of the sunset than the wavelengths of its light: more in human loyalty and affection than instincts which make for the survival of the race: more in a great service of worship and praise than a hedonistic illusion which makes its participants feel comfortable. At worst the atheist is entirely selfish; at best vainly striving for evolutionary progress, forgetting that on his view that very progress has been responsible for man's present wickedness and his repeated attempts to destroy himself.

Dualism is a more subtle rival to the Christian view of God. It accepts an eternal supernatural world—a principle of Good—even, maybe, a personal God, but denies that He is the Creator of all. Co-existent and co-eternal with Him is a principle of Evil, usually identified with the matter of which the universe is composed, or the primitive substance on which Good has worked to produce the world as we experience it. This is a tempting philosophy and is held by many in one form or other. It offers a ready-made answer to the Problem of Evil. It fits in very nicely with that facile view of man's wickedness which makes it merely the unfortunate entail of his animal origin. But it is important to realize that Christianity is mercilessly opposed to it. To begin with, it is cruel. It invites deliberate material suffering for spiritual gain. It offers no certainty that Good will ever triumph, or that God can ever control matter as He wills. It is denied on page after page of Scripture. God saw everything that He had made, and it was very good (Gen. i, 31). The earth is the Lord's and the fulness thereof (Ps. xxiv, 1). In the beginning was the Word. . . . All things were made by Him (John i, 1, 3). In a bold passage, Isaiah tells us of God: "I create evil" (Isa. xlv, 7), by which he means that the law which joins suffering to sin is under God's control and will. Evil is not eternal; it has been allowed to take place by God, but He will triumph over it, and God will be all in all (1 Cor. xv, 28).

Polytheism, though it can claim the allegiance of great sections of the human race, affects us less in the West than the other alternatives. It resolves the observed complexity of the world into a multitude of individual deities, each, so to speak, with his or her own axe to grind. The existing tensions in the moral realm are identified with the conflicts of divine wills; the association of immorality with this kind of religion, to which history consistently testifies, can hardly surprise us. Man here makes gods in his own image, and falls victim to the temptation of finding divine support for his own failures. "They that make them are like unto them," says the psalmist (Ps. cxv, 8), and reason corroborates the fact. If man defies his instinctive consciousness of a Supreme Being and a final moral law, multiplying gods to himself after the likeness of his warring passions, he cannot help growing like the degraded deities he has blinded himself into worshipping.

Pantheism identifies God with His creation. It is true that God pervades and sustains His universe, but Pantheism denies Him any existence external to it. He is the World-soul, the Mind of which the Mind-stuff of the world is made, the aggregate of all our consciousnesses. It is not very satisfying, but the thinking of many is unconsciously governed by it. It shows itself in the senseless rush "back to nature": the sentimental desire for harmony with one's environment: the purely pagan recrudescence of astrology.

What does the Christian say to this? He claims quite simply and directly that God is personal, and His will brought the world into being. First, God is personal. As the Bishop of Bradford puts it,[1] God is He and not It. This does not mean God is like us; it means we are to this extent like God. This is implied by the phrase in Genesis: "God created man in His own image" (Gen. i, 27). Our personality is a dim shadow, a picture in an earthly medium, of the Personality of God. The glories of human personality at its best—its unity, its integrity, its individuality, its character, its reason, its volition —are derived from a Person who thus possesses them all, albeit to a degree and of a quality infinitely removed from our own. As such He is utterly distinct from His creation, wholly other than any created thing. He is Himself, or in His own words to Moses, "I am that I am" (Exod. iii, 14).

Secondly, God by His own will brought the world into being. He spake and it was done. Before that divine command went forth, outside the confines of time and space, Himself calling both into being, stands the Eternal I AM. No other Being in the world frustrated Him, for none existed until He willed them to be. No primeval matter confronted Him, or thwarted Him by its refractibility, for there was none until He spoke the creative word. His power maintains the universe which His power created.[2]

We must notice that we are not here concerned with *how* God made the world. This is a fascinating study which man is called to undertake. "The works of the Lord are great, sought out of all them that have pleasure therein" (Ps. cxi, 2). It is only when man forgets that God made it that he is in danger of making nonsense of the story. We shall be thinking later of the authority for the Christian of the revelation found in the Bible, but it must suffice here to say that that revelation

[1] *What the Church Teaches*, Penguin.
[2] It is significant that modern science tends more and more to find the ultimate elements of the structure of the world in units of power or force-centres. The world appears to us as an assemblage of gravitational and electrical fields of force whose centres, or singularities as the scientist says, are protons, neutrons, electrons, and maybe others. But the really fundamental things seem to be the force-fields of whose nature we know nothing, but whose effects we are able to observe. Does this illustrate for us and help us to understand the words of Hebrews i, 3: "upholding all things by the word of His power"?

seems to claim two important things about the process: (i) it consisted of a number of definite successive acts of God (read, for example, Gen. i and Ps. civ); and (ii) the creation of human personality was a unique and specific act or event. Whatever science may purport to say about the origin of man's body (and many theories have had a short innings only to be bowled out by a stubborn fact), we can have no doubt as Christians that his spiritual nature, which distinguishes him from the beasts and makes him capable of fellowship with and accountable to God, is a divine gift miraculously implanted. It is not a growth from the past, the evolved consciousness of animal ancestors. It would appear to be inseparable from the whole of man's non-material nature. Many, including the author, believe that his body also was a specific creation of God, but this may not be the only meaning of Genesis ii, 7, nor is it an essential of Christian belief. A short note on the question of Evolution will be found in Appendix I.

What does all this mean to the Christian? It means a very great deal. The Christian believes in Jesus Christ and has learnt through Him to call God Father. He lives and moves in his Father's world. He draws his breath in his Father's air. His body is sustained by his Father's power. He is a prince in his Father's kingdom, an heir on his Father's estate. The world to him is a book by which he learns of home, a picture of the truths of the spirit, a witness of his Father's providence and care. He enjoys the good things of the world as well as any man, indeed better, for he looks beyond the transient satisfaction which they can give to his Father's right hand, where there are pleasures for evermore.

He finds pledges of his Father's goodness in the beauty of the world about him; it is a gift coming down from above, alike in the object of beauty and the faculty to appreciate it. Experience of life becomes to him something of the vision of God which it was to the Psalmist: "the voice of the Lord breaketh the cedars . . . , and in His temple everything saith 'Glory'." (Ps. xxix, 5, 9, R.V.) Whether it be the vision of the land of far distances, the sound of the symphony in his ears, the prick of the rock beneath his fingers, the taste of the fruits of the earth, the scents of evening, the warmth of the sun, the sting of the rain, the roar of the sea, the swell of the hills—all speak to him of God who giveth us richly all things to enjoy.

He thanks God, too, that "He setteth the solitary in families"—for human love and companionship, for home and family, for the laws of his physical being, for the joy of work and of healthy exercise—these also are the gifts of his Maker, who doeth all things well. In Robert Herrick's words he may say:

> "All these, and better Thou dost send
> Me, to this end,
> That I should render for my part
> A thankfull heart."

But the Christian is a realist. God's book of nature has its stern pages; God's Fatherhood is not indulgence. Tempest and earthquake, swamp and desert, the strange twistedness of parasitism and disease remind him that this world is not a Paradise. The book of Nature is a parable of the book of Man; Man expelled from the Garden, made foul by crime, tortured by pain, destroying himself in internecine strife. And both books speak of his own heart, a well of wickedness which gets deeper the more he plumbs it. Nature, history, human personality, all alike are traversed by the most tremendous paradoxes which are not resolvable by any facile Dualism. We may be assured by our belief in God as Creator that He will ultimately triumph. We cannot imagine that He would allow to have more than a temporary existence anything which appears to oppose His purposes as Evil does in the world as we see it. The Christian doctrine of Creation carries with it as a corollary the doctrine of God's sovereignty and of His final victory. How that sovereignty is displayed and how that victory is won is the theme of the following chapters.

CHAPTER II

GOD MOVES IN HISTORY

THERE is a very striking and significant difference between the view of God as conceived by the highest and noblest Greek Philosophy, and that revealed to the Hebrew in the Old Testament. The one pictures God as man would have Him be: perfectly holy in His majesty indeed, but aloof, austere, alone, wholly indifferent to man's struggles and man's sin. To the Hebrew prophet God reveals Himself as holy and just; demanding man's obedience and co-operation.

To the Greek at his best, God is the One, the Prime Cause, as He is to the Christian. But He is intangible, impersonal, the πρῶτον κίνουν ἀκίνητον, moving to create, but unmoved by creation's agonies. History to him is thus, in Dr. Whale's striking phrase, but a pathetic fountain, aiming at heaven and falling in tears. There is here no moral compulsion, no thought of guilt or redemption; neither hope for man's aspirations nor discomfort for his pride.

The moment we open the pages of our Old Testament we are conscious of being in a different world. Here is no vague philosophical speculation, no tenuous metaphysics; here is the rough and tumble of human history, the splendid and the sordid side by side. We are faced at once with the realities of life. God, we learn, is concerned with cruelty to animals, with just weights and measures, with oppression of the poor, tenure of land, and a thousand other requirements of social justice.[1] Can this really be a revelation of God, and even if it were to the ancient Hebrew, is it of any value to the Christian of today?

We must admit to begin with that this picture of God is eminently practical and suited to our needs. There is something surprisingly modern about it all; Isaiah's strictures might well have referred to the internal moral decline and

---

[1] *See* e.g. Lev. xxii, 28; Deut. xxiii-xxv; Amos viii, 4-6; Mic. ii, 1-2.

vacillating foreign policies of our own day, and in a war against tyranny Habakkuk's words sound startlingly up to date.[1] But as Christians we feel there is more than this. We are faced with the fact that our Master whose name we bear and whom we profess to follow, treated the Old Testament as God's authoritative Word, and the prophets as the revealers of His will to man. Let us see what this implies.

Why did man need such a revelation? Why could he not discover God for himself by his own reasoning and his own acts of worship? The full answer to this question must be postponed until we come to think more specifically of man. Suffice it here to say that man by wilful independence became estranged from his Maker, and had to learn by long and devious paths the way back to God. It is plain to all that *something* has gone wrong with man and the world about him, and that he could learn little about God's real nature either from himself or his surroundings. If he is to find God, then God must take the initiative and reveal Himself. The basis of Christian belief is just this—*God has done so.*

To Christ and to the Christian the Old Testament is not merely a record of Jewish religion, or the growth of Hebrew ideas about God; it is God's revelation of Himself to man. Of course, there is progress; God is not like a foolish teacher who gives to beginners an advanced treatise quite beyond their powers. He teaches by stages suited to the capacity of man to learn. But He is throughout the Teacher; He controls the curriculum, and He never teaches the false which will have to be unlearnt later.

Let us then reverently open our Bibles and learn how He has set about it. We are struck at once by the fact that much of the book is history, though not in the ordinary secular sense. The record is biographical and personal, revealing men as God sees them, and bringing home to the reader the consequences of sin and the fruits of righteousness. God has taught man by His actions in man's own experience—the first pages God wrote in the revelation were the pages of human history,

[1] *See* Isa. vii, 3-9, xix, xx, xxviii-xxxi; Habakkuk, the whole book, especially i, 5-11, ii,6-14.

recorded and interpreted for us by His faithful servants. We trace man from the Garden, driven out because of his sin, learning through the Flood of the consequences of wickedness, and of the holiness and grace of his Creator; and then after a new start declining again into sin and idolatry. We then read how God takes one man, Abraham, and from him one race, the Hebrews, and plans through them to reveal Himself and to bless every family on earth. We learn of Abraham's personal education in the path of faith; of that of his sons; of the nation's trials in Egypt and in the wilderness, forging them in the furnace of affliction into the sword of God. To this nation, God's chosen channel of blessing to man, He gives His law: His standard of worship, of personal and social ethics, of public life and hygiene. He commands His servant Moses to preserve this law for us, and Christ claimed that it spoke of Him and He came personally to fulfil it. Finally we see God teaching His people by their relations with heathen nations—learning the bitter fruits of disobedience and the victories which God gives to faith.

Then there is much ceremony and ritual. Much of the Law of Moses in Exodus and Leviticus is concerned with worship and sacrifice, feast and fast, atonement and purification. The Jew is taught in marvellous pictures, only fully to be understood long afterwards, the heinousness of sin and the path of sacrifice by which alone man may return to God. But, says the hasty modern reader, of what possible use to us is all this? Worse—is it not all very crude and horrible, this "religion of the shambles"? Before we pass judgment we must remember three things. First, there was nothing cruel about it. No animals were burnt or impaled alive as in many heathen cults. Human sacrifice was an abomination. Cruelty was ruthlessly forbidden and severely punished. Most of the flesh was used as meat for the priests and people. Some of the sacrifices in the wilderness were merely the recognition of God as the giver of life before an animal was slain for food (Lev. xvii; Deut. xii). The priest was the recognized butcher and public health officer. Secondly, it was necessary for the Jew to be taught that sin is costly, that God is holy, and that death is the gateway to life, and faith the key to forgiveness. Thirdly, the Christian Church has always followed the guidance of the writer to the Hebrews in seeing in the tabernacle, the temple and its ritual, wonderful prophetic illustrations of the work of Jesus Christ on the Cross.

Turning from the Law, we come to the Prophets.[1] This second great division of the Old Testament includes much that we should call history. For God's revelation of Himself in history has been interpreted to us by God's spokesmen the prophets. They saw that God has not held aloof from man, but that He still holds the reins of government, and His judgments are in the earth. They tell us repeatedly that God honours those who honour Him, and that national prosperity depends on obedience to His will. They are insistent that God has chosen Israel for a purpose, to be the channel of His revelation to the world. If His people fail in that purpose by declension into idolatry or by moral decline they have broken the terms of their covenant with God and are to be charged with the sin of unfaithfulness. Such action persisted in can bring only punishment. God uses wicked men and nations as His tools, and He will carry out His unshakable intention of creating for Himself a nation that will serve Him and live in righteousness. But there are at first hints and then more definite prophecies that this will not be until the Perfect Servant of Jehovah is revealed, who will Himself atone for the sin of His people, and through whom the new nation shall be created. The consistent testimony of the apostles of Jesus Christ in the New Testament is that in Him all these longings, foreshadowings, and promises have found their fulfilment.

The third section of the Old Testament is the Sacred Writings, or the Psalms and the Wisdom books, from Job to Solomon's Song, with a few other books. Here we find the wisdom and the aspirations, the worship and the perplexities of great servants of God, expressed in language which

---

[1] These are the Hebrew divisions of the O.T. as referred to, for instance, in Luke xxiv, 44. In our English Bibles "the Writings" come between the historical and prophetical parts of "the Prophets."

has proved an enduring vehicle for the inmost emotions of the hearts of saints in all ages.

For the Christian, then, the Old Testament is no dull history of an Eastern people; it is instinct with the voice of God. In it he sees the invincible progress of God's great purposes; the story of man's failure and God's perseverance; the steps by which God has taught man of Himself and forwarded His great plan to redeem him; the word that has come to him by God's messengers, with its insistence on God's standard of right and wrong and with its promise of a triumphant future.

This Book makes inspiring reading in these modern days. It reminds us of two vital truths which we are tempted to forget. The first is that life is a whole, a unity, and that God is concerned not only with our devotions and religious exercises, but with every department of our activities. There is no division of life for the Christian into sacred and secular. There was none for the loyal Israelite. God is the Lord of all life, and man can fulfil his part in creation and live his life fully and effectively only in so far as he submits to divine control. My relation to my neighbour is not only a matter of sociology and economics, of personal or political expediency; it is something about which the moral law of God makes vital pronouncements. David, after committing the crimes of adultery and murder, thereby foully abusing the privileges of kingship and grievously wronging the people committed to his rule, can yet cry out to God in his great psalm of repentance: "Against Thee, Thee only, have I sinned, and done that which is evil in Thy sight" (Ps. li, 4). With him his relationship with God preceded and included all other relationships.

The second great truth is that God is sovereign in human history. We are tempted to think that man's wickedness can frustrate or delay God's decrees, but the Old Testament repeatedly tells us that this is not so. The wrath of man, says the psalmist, shall turn to God's praise (Ps. lxxvi, 10). The Lord is King, be the earth never so unquiet (Ps. xcix, 1, Prayer Book Version). The hearts of kings are in His hand (Prov. xxi, 1); Cyrus shall do all His pleasure (Isa. xliv, 28);

Assyria is a rod in God's hand, and carries out, all un-consciously, God's charge (Isa. x, 5-7). Even Nebuchadnezzar confesses that the Most High ruleth in the kingdom of men and giveth it to whomsoever He will (Dan. iv, 17).[1] The fact is that although God is not the author of evil, and the cruel tyrant, for example, is entirely responsible for his crimes, yet God can use the actions of such men to forward His own plans. Simply put, He allows evil to be its own check, to overstep itself and bring its own destruction. This is a law of God's world, and He can effectively put it into operation because He sees the end from the beginning. He is the Creator of time as well as of space. We can conceive of events occurring together and interacting in many parts of space (though action at a distance remains obscure to the philosopher, however the physicist may be able to picture it). But we are tied to a progressive temporal experience, and we are apt to forget that this is a property of our own consciousness, and not an essential property of time itself. To the Creator there is but one eternal Now—all things are present to His sight. Much of the paradox of this complex world is resolved by this simple fact; or rather the complexity and the profundity is thereby transferred from the creation to the nature of God Himself, and we are more satisfied to leave it there. He knows the hearts of all men, and all our desires are laid open to His view. Therefore our free choices are seen by Him as a whole—they are part of the data of His eternal mind, if we may put it in such blatantly human language, and He is thus able to control their consequences and even, by control of the stimuli to which we are all continually subject, to modify or intensify the choice which we ourselves are responsible to direct.

[1] There are passages such as Num. xiv, 34 (margin) and 1 Sam. xv, 11 which seem to imply a change of purpose on God's part, but Samuel's own words in 1 Sam. xv, 29, paralleled by Num. xxiii, 19, preclude us from a literal understanding of what is plainly an anthropomorphism. The truth seems to be that God's *decrees* are unalterable; His *will* may mean only His wishes or longing desires for us, which, of course, we may fail to attain. But Scripture teaches us that His plan allows for and includes that failure. For further comments see Chap. IV below, and also Guillebaud, *Some Moral Difficulties of the Bible*, Chaps. IV and V, for a much fuller discussion.

Thus, in the Old Testament, actions, which we might today hesitate so to ascribe, are ascribed to the divine will; God hardens Pharaoh's heart (Exod. ix, 12 *et al.*), He sends an evil spirit upon Saul (1 Sam. xvi, 14), and a spirit of falsehood into the unfaithful prophets (1 Kings xxii, 19-23). If calamity befalls a city, surely the Lord hath done it (Amos iii, 6). But it is a shallow view to reject this as crude; the vision of the Hebrew went deeper than the idea of a vengeful God: he saw that although man was responsible for his own evil choices, yet God was Lord of the world and permitted or intensified the consequences of those choices in accordance with His eternal law, "Whatsoever a man soweth, that shall he also reap" (Gal. vi, 7). In temporal experience Pharaoh hardened his own heart before God hardened it, and God used this wicked attitude to demonstrate His superiority to the gods of Egypt and to deepen His people's faith in His power to deliver them. Man may rage and devils oppose, but God's purposes move steadily forward to the coming of His Christ. Humanly speaking, it all appeared a stupendous failure when He was crucified, but Peter can declare in daring but convincing paradox, "Him, being delivered up by the determinate counsel and foreknowledge of God, ye by the hand of lawless men did crucify and slay" (Acts ii, 23, R.V.), and "God hath made Him both Lord and Christ, this Jesus whom ye crucified" (Acts ii, 36, R.V.). If God is sovereign here, on this the darkest day of human history; if out of this unspeakable crime He can bring to man the greatest blessing he has ever received; then nothing is too hard for Him and no situation is beyond His control.

This is a great mystery, and, of course, it is by no means confined to Christianity. Much in the world speaks of plan and purpose and a beneficent Designer; yet always there is the sinister possibility of human hostility to the plan, and always man's conscience charges him with responsibility for his errors. Yet we refuse to believe that an almighty Creator has simply let the reins of government slip. Christian doctrine is at least paradoxical enough to be true, and we can only be content firmly to hold the twin truths of God's sovereignty and man's responsibility, remembering that the greatest minds of the. ages have confessed themselves baffled by this very proble m

Man moves in history, now wisely and with foresight, now blindly and foolishly; now actuated by noblest motives, now by selfish greed. But God moves too, and step by step history makes progress towards the fulfilment of His sublime purposes as He revealed them by the mouth of His holy prophets since the world began.[1]

[1] For a note on the miraculous element in the O.T., see Appendix II.

CHAPTER III

GOD COMES IN JESUS CHRIST

ON one occasion, during our Lord's last week of earthly life. His enemies tried to inveigle Him into an indictable offence by demanding the authority with which He did His miracles. He refused to give them a direct or immediate reply, but went on to give the real answer in a parable of the profoundest significance. This is the so-called Parable of the Wicked Husbandmen (Mark xii, 1-9). In language strikingly and intentionally similar to the Song of the Vineyard in Isaiah v, which every Jew recognized as a picture of his own nation, He described a man who let his vineyard to husbandmen while he himself went elsewhere. The lease, however, did not include the fruits, and the owner sent servants from time to time to collect them. One and all were cruelly and shamefully treated by the husbandmen; some were killed, others sent back empty. At last he sent his only son, thinking they would at least respect a member of the family. But the men, thinking by killing the heir to gain the inheritance for themselves, slew him and cast him out. What would you do, He said, if you were the owner? "He will come and destroy the husbandmen, and will give the vineyard unto others."

The Pharisees did not fail to see His meaning—they knew He had spoken the parable against them. The claim He made was stupendous and challenging; He was God's *only* Son, His unique revelation: He was God's *last* messenger to His people; He knew full well the end He was facing, and He pronounced the dire consequences to the unfaithful Israel. They rejected that claim, with conscious self-righteousness considering it blasphemous; but history proved the truth of what He said. Within a week He was crucified and risen; within two months three thousand were joyfully accepting His challenge and beginning to yield the fruits of the vineyard; within forty years Jerusalem was razed to the ground, its temple defiled, its proud inhabitants scattered to the corners of the Roman empire. Christians with one voice have endorsed His claim and accepted the testimony of history and of His Resurrection. "God", say they, "who at sundry times and in divers manners spake in time past unto the fathers by the prophets hath in these last days spoken unto us by His Son" (Heb. i, 1-2).

Jesus Christ, then, is God's last word to man. He is the culmination and the explanation of the Old Testament revelation, the final and complete revelation of God to man.

By making this claim He authenticates the words of His predecessors the prophets—they are the servants whom God sent to His husbandmen—and at the same time He brands as counterfeit all subsequent or independent supposed revelation. While therefore "God has yet more light to break forth from His Word" we must not twist His Word into a meaning which is opposed to the supreme revelation in Jesus Christ. Neither can we accept the "revelations" of spiritism, or the claim of Mohammed to be a prophet of God. How did God set about giving us this revelation of Himself? He began in the most unexpected way imaginable. He began with the baby son of a peasant woman, born in a hay-rack in the courtyard of an Eastern inn. We might have expected Him to begin with some youth in the prime of life, with a prince or nobleman, a man of wealth and influence, of culture and learning. But that was not God's way: He began at the beginning, and He thereby gave us a complete human life from birth to manhood. More than that, He did not, as it were, infuse Deity into an existing human life; by taking humanity into His own Nature He made a new thing—a life which from the beginning was both human and divine. Nor did He take man at his boasted best and add to him the difference between that and Godhead; He sent His Son into the everyday strata of human life and showed that there in the trivial round of daily experience God could be revealed.

The Incarnation of Jesus Christ is a staggering event; it has been the inspiration of man's wonder and rejoicing in all ages, for it has brought eternity into the confines of human life: "the great God of Heaven is come to the birth." But we must be clear as to its meaning. It is an act of God in self-revelation in the only terms which man can fully understand—the terms of human personality. *By itself* it does not imply that human nature is nigh unto the divine or can by this fact alone be made more godlike. These things are true in the sense that man was made originally in the image of God, and it is God's purpose to restore man to that state, but the Incarnation does not prove, as it has been sometimes held to, that man *as he is now* has in him the "spark of the divine", nor can it by itself empower man to live the life that Christ lived.

The facts of Christ's birth take a small place in the Gospels when compared with the accounts of His death; the finger of the New Testament points to His Cross as the central point of the Revelation, and we shall alter this emphasis to our spiritual loss.

With this caveat, then, let us stand again in wonder before this amazing act of our God. The very condescension of it may disincline us to believe it. Can it be really true that this despised Jew, this humble carpenter, this poor preacher, is indeed God the Son? This same question baffled his contemporaries. Can any good thing, they said, come out of Nazareth? Let us see what led those who knew Him best to accept His claims.

First and foremost among His credentials we must set His sinless life. Here is a Man who walked the pathway of human vicissitudes, whom none could ever honestly accuse of any departure from the highest: who spent His life in doing good: whose unique personality appealed unmistakably to all who met Him: whose flaming purity challenged every mean and ignoble thing in His presence. In open court He could demand of His bitterest enemies: "Which of you convinceth me of sin?" (John viii, 46); the officers sent to take Him had to confess: "Never man spake like this man" (John vii, 46); even Judas, His betrayer, testified to His innocence (Matt. xxvii, 4); Pilate, the shrewd Roman procurator, found no fault in Him; the hardened centurion at Calvary confessed:

"Truly, this was the Son of God" (Mark xv, 39). Even more significant is the positive side of His holy character; the balanced soberness of His life, His sensitiveness to atmosphere, the aptness of His sayings, His words of comfort and encouragement, His well-placed rebukes calling to holiness, His homeliness and sympathy; all bear out the truth of John's testimony to Him as "full of grace and truth" (John i, 14).

Then there is the evidence of His miracles; His healing of diseases of all kinds at a touch; His feeding of 5,000 and then 4,000 from a few loaves and fishes; His stilling of the storm; His raising to life of the daughter of Jairus, the widow's son, the full-grown Lazarus, four days dead.

Then there are His own personal claims. At first made only to intimates, but then in the closing weeks more publicly declared, they are unmistakable. He claimed to forgive sins, to cast out devils, to have existed before Abraham, to modify the Law of Moses, to fulfil the Old Testament Scriptures, to be the future judge of mankind, to be the Messiah, the Son of the Blessed, to be one with His Father who sent Him. Either He was mad or wickedly deceitful, or else His claims are true. "Aut deus," says Anselm, "aut non bonus homo." His gentleness and sympathy, His self-control and dignity utterly preclude the alternative of madness; His absolute sinlessness and His open, transparent character give the lie to any suggestion of deceit. Even without the final demonstration in His Resurrection we should have to confess Him as our Lord and God. Of this great truth God has given assurance to all men in raising Him from the dead. This is the final incontestable ground of our assurance, the unshakable testimony of His disciples, the fact above all others which led to the deepening conviction that this is in very deed God manifest in the flesh.

How did His followers express this conviction, and what were its implications? To begin with, there was a secret which His mother Mary had treasured in her heart, which could not in the nature of things have been made part of His public evidence earlier, but now became deeply significant and recalled a mysterious saying of the great prophet Isaiah. The chain of human generation had been broken in the case of Jesus of Nazareth, and He had no human father: Joseph was not married to Mary until afterwards. Two independent witnesses tell us this, and the truth could only have been learnt from Joseph and Mary themselves. Mary had received an angelic message that the power of the Most High would overshadow her, and that holy thing which should be born of her should be called the Son of God (Luke i, 35).

Christians have always seen in this fact of the Virgin Birth of our Lord a profound significance. It gives added meaning to the fact of His being truly God and truly Man; and it marks Him out from all other men by attributing His birth to direct divine initiative. God has here come down to earth, and has chosen to be born as a human baby. Mary, the humble recipient of this amazing gift, is indeed most highly favoured, and, in her womanhood and motherhood, is greatly honoured of God. Yet in humility she confesses that she is but God's servant, and depends on God to be her Saviour, for she is truly human and her nature is the same as ours. It is through God's power that the entail of sin is broken, and Jesus derived from Mary no inclination to sin and no corruption or weakness in His personality. This is the miracle in the spiritual world of which the Virgin Birth is the physical counterpart.[1]

Then in their first public preaching His disciples began to realize that Jesus was the Christ, the fulfilment of many of the Old Testament prophecies, and not exclusively of those which the Jews had referred to the Messiah. "This," says Peter in almost the first words of his first public utterance, "This is that" (Acts ii, 16), and his words are pregnant with meaning. *This* which you now see, he says, is *that* which the prophets sought after. That to which all the Old Testament pointed is now here; this is the culminating revelation; the eternal life of God, dimly perceived in law and vision, has now invaded the world of men.

Nor was it long before they convincedly proclaimed that

[1] For a detailed analysis of the evidence for the Virgin Birth, see J. Gresham Machen, *The Virgin Birth* (Marshall, Morgan & Scott).

this was none other than God Himself who had walked and talked in their midst. This was naturally a great stumbling-block to the strict and rigid Jew, with his high insistence on absolute monotheism, but the force of the revelation was such that nothing less would satisfy the facts. To interpret this and formulate a full *doctrine* of the Trinity was the work of the Church through three centuries and more of bitter controversies, and we cannot stop to consider it yet. But of the *facts* the New Testament writers are clear. Paul tells us that Christ is over all, God blessed for ever (Rom. ix, 5), and in Him dwelleth all the fulness of the Godhead bodily (Col. ii, 9). The writer to the Hebrews ascribes to Him the words of Psalm xlv: "Thy throne, O God, is for ever and ever" (Heb. i, 8), and St. John gives us the profound words, "In the beginning was the Word; and the Word was with God, and the Word was God. . . . And the Word became flesh" (John i, 1, 14, R.V.).

The implications of this are far-reaching, and we can only touch on them here. Christ Jesus is the Word of God—a fact which includes, among other ideas, the thought that He is both the eternal Reason of the Godhead, the Mind behind the universe, and the expression of that Mind in a form which is intelligible to man. This invests the record of His life with more than ordinary significance, for through the pages of the Gospels we follow the feet of God Incarnate. Further, it makes His teaching trustworthy and authoritative. Attempts have been made to minimize this by a theory that when He divested Himself of the splendour of the Godhead He also laid aside His omniscience and, as man, adopted His contemporaries' ideas which may not have been correct. There is a subtle confusion here. Of course, as man He had to learn; in that mysterious relation between mind and brain of which we know so little, He went through the normal process of "increasing in wisdom and stature." But He did not lay aside His infallibility, or He would have ceased to be God. He voluntarily accepted limitations, but it is impossible to suppose He voluntarily allowed Himself to be deceived and so to mislead others, for that would be sin. On one occasion

(Matt. xxiv, 36) He stated He did not know something, because it would not have been in man's interest for Him to have known and passed it on. But, as has been said before, the remarkable thing is that He knew He did not know, and said so, and this increases the authority of those things He did know and say. We might perhaps put it that as God He had power to call into His human consciousness any fact which He desired, but that He normally chose to do so by the ordinary process of learning. But we must not press this, for it is impossible to separate the divine and the human in His personality in this way.

By His life and His words, then, He reveals to us His Father. "Show us the Father," said Philip. "Have I been so long time with you, and yet hast thou not known Me," was His reply (John xiv, 8, 9).

What do we learn about God from Him? Supremely, we learn that God is love. He is full of compassion for our suffering and longs to win us in spite of our sin. Indeed, He sent Jesus Christ for this very purpose. We learn, too, that God is holy and requires holiness and truth in the motives of man's heart, as well as in his actions. Hypocrisy arouses His anger, and He will never condone sin and moral failure; He will not let us go content with any standard short of the highest. Then He shows us that God's plan is to embrace the whole world, and His message must be sent to all. The Jew's day of privilege is past, and the purpose of his being chosen by God and given so many privileges has now been completed. We learn also that those who come to God by Christ may call Him Father, though others who reject Him are sternly called "children of the devil". But we learn more than can be put into any classification; we see, as far as it can be seen in the medium of a human life, the whole character of God. God is like Jesus Christ: "he that hath seen Me hath seen the Father." Above all we see this revelation in its culminating event, at the Cross and Resurrection of our Lord Jesus Christ. What He was doing there, and what it means for man we shall consider in the chapters which follow.

SUMMARY OF SECTION I

The essentials of Christian belief about God may be summarized thus:

(1) God is *eternally self-existent*. He owes His being to no other, and all else owes its being to Him.

(2) God is *personal*. He can be thought of as thinking, willing, loving, hating. He can be revealed in terms of the human personality of Jesus Christ.

(3) God is *sovereign*. What we call natural law is the expression of His power and orderliness. Miracles demonstrate His control of His own laws. In human history His directing hand is seen. Evil is subordinated to His purposes, wherein He will ultimately triumph openly.

(4) God is *holy*. All that He made was good, and He cannot tolerate imperfection, either in man or in the rest of creation.

(5) God is *love*. Love is the essence of His holy character, and impelled Him to plan to win man back to Himself. This love is perfectly revealed to us in Jesus Christ.

(6) God *speaks by revelation*. First He speaks through the Old Testament, which points forward to Christ and derives its authority from Him; then finally He reveals Himself fully in His Son.

GOD'S PLAN TO MEET MAN'S NEED

CHAPTER IV

THE PLIGHT OF HUMANITY

FROM contemplating God's revelation of Himself in creation, in history, and in Jesus Christ, we turn to consider His revelation of ourselves, that is, of His creature, man. We shall not find the picture flattering or the investigation comfortable. God respects no man's person and panders to no man's pride. We must be prepared for painful discoveries and disagreeable truths. Many would prefer to disregard some of the more uncomfortable statements, though the shattering of ideals and illusions consequent on two world wars has caused much revision of opinion. It was once popular to believe that man's failings were merely relics of supposed earlier stages in his evolution. It was easy, when the full tide of industrial and imperial progress was flowing, to imagine that such progress would continue indefinitely, and to forget the ever-present peril of the hidden reef of human sin. Now that the vessel of humanity has well-nigh foundered on cruel rocks, men are more disposed to turn again to the old chart which reveals the true channel to their desired haven.

What then does the Bible say? To begin with, it gives man a place of honour and dignity which seems at first sight to bear out man's own estimate of himself. (Not that man's own estimate may be worth very much, for it is scarcely unbiased, and he has very little data for comparison.) "What is man," says David, "that Thou art mindful of him, and the son of man that Thou visitest him? For Thou hast made him but little lower than God, and crownest him with glory and honour. Thou madest him to have dominion over the works of Thy hands; Thou hast put all things under his feet" (Ps.

viii. 4-6 R.V.). But can this be really true—man, ever and anon the slave of his own passions, made to have dominion over all creation? How is it that this creature, the noblest of God's creation, can yet descend so low? Gifted with powers of mind immeasurably transcending those of his fellow-creatures in the animal kingdom, with a personality capable of such devotion to them that our Lord could compare Himself to the good shepherd who gives his life for the sheep; yet he sinks to depths of cruelty and bestiality of which they could never be guilty and whose very name is a libel on the beasts. There is stark tragedy here, and in our more lucid moments we do not need Scripture to reveal it to us. But for explanation it is to Scripture we must turn.

To learn what God has to say to us on this important matter we must go back to a very ancient story that has come to us from man's earliest days on earth. There in the early chapters of Genesis we read a narrative of elemental simplicity, but of the profoundest significance. It tells us in the first place that when God first breathed into man the spirit of life (in whatever way his body was given him, it matters not here), thereby creating his self-consciousness and his personality, He made him perfectly fitted to do God's will. In the words of the Bible, man became a living soul (Gen. ii, 7). Further, in his pristine state, man bore out the truth of David's words we have quoted from the eighth psalm; he was made to have dominion over the rest of creation.

A difficulty arises here which deserves passing mention. In these days of evolutionary philosophy, 'primitive' means 'crude', and moral and material progress have been largely identified. Careful investigation, however, goes to support the view that man's religion degenerated from monotheism to polytheism, and we are not justified in the absence of evidence in saying that primeval man was spiritually or morally inferior to his present-day descendants.[1] He had, of course, everything to learn; but he enjoyed unbroken communion with God, which invested him with an authority over himself and the lower creation which would arouse our envy and amaze-

[1] *See* e.g. Zwemer, *The Origin of Religion.*

ment could he stand among us and make himself known.[1]
God thus made man "in His own image", giving him a
personality modelled on His own and which was to find its
fullest expression in self-surrender to the will of the Creator.

Man was thus originally capable of a spiritual growth and
achievement through his union with God which is now quite
beyond his grasp. So far from his failures being relics of his
animal origin which he has not yet outgrown, his very successes
and all his most admirable qualities are only his because of
that original creation which made him in the image of God.
It is because he shows evidence of being made for a purpose
greater than he is able to perform, because he knows that his
proper function is one which he cannot attain, that his
failure and his inadequacy are so tragic and so contemptible.
For since he is a moral being, his proper function in life is not
a mere biological necessity for survival; it is incumbent on
him with the pressure of a moral imperative, so that he says
to himself not only "This is the thing for which I was made,"
but "This is the thing I *ought* to do—which I owe as a debt to
my Creator." He knows, therefore, when he is honest with
himself, that he is responsible for his position, and the feeling
of *guilt* will not be far from his thoughts. He has not responded
to the righteous and loving demand of a personal God.

It is reasonable to inquire more closely into the cause of
this state of affairs. The story we are considering goes on to
speak of the temptation offered to Eve, the first woman, to
doubt God's benevolence towards man and to disobey His
explicit command with regard to eating the fruit of the tree
of knowledge of good and evil. The being who suggested this
to her is described as the Serpent. Eve accepted the suggestion,
and persuaded her husband to join her in eating the fruit,
with the most momentous consequences for her own psychical
nature and for the whole future of mankind. Death was the
penalty of her act, man's fellowship with God was broken, and
sorrow and toil became his lifelong burdens.

The story is frequently regarded as myth, that is to say, as

[1] For a full treatment of this point, see a section of considerable interest
in C. S. Lewis' *The Problem of Pain*, pp. 60-67 (Centenary Press).

a folk-tale which seeks to explain a puzzling state of affairs by a dramatic presentation of its origin as an event affecting heroic figures who are in fact mere personifications. In much the same way the classical story of Demeter and Persephone explains the annual onset of winter to give place in its turn to spring, and, to cite a popular fairy tale, the problem of the triumph of the wicked is resolved in Cinderella. It is clear that St. Paul thought otherwise (2 Cor. xi, 3; 1 Tim. ii, 14 *et al.*), and we may presume from Matt. xix, 5, and John viii, 44, that our Lord did also. Its primitive character commands our attention, and though we are, perhaps, to regard some of its details as figurative, we need not hesitate to affirm that it represents historic fact. There must needs have been some occasion which led to man's fall into sin, a state which we now see and which we cannot believe was that of his original creation, and the Genesis account of this occasion has the merits of simplicity and verisimilitude and is of a piece with the rest of Scripture. For many Christians, including the writer, the testimony of Christ would clinch the question, but we have tried to show that on other grounds the historicity of the account is not unreasonable.

There is no doubt of the value of its spiritual truth. Evil is present in God's world in the person of the serpent, who is either the unconscious instrument or the pictorial representation of the Adversary of God whom the Hebrews knew as Satan and the Greeks as the Devil (Rev. xii, 9). (How he conceived this implacable animosity against God is only hinted at, though we may be sure it was not always so; and if, as many Christians have felt, passages like Isaiah xiv, 12ff., and Ezekiel xxviii, 12-19, point to the evil powers behind earthly tyrants, we may conclude that his sin also was that which he induced in Eve, the pride of a creature in independence of its Creator.) This spiritual being, who has his agents in the world of spiritual realities which is all about us, though we know so little of it, has been permitted by God to remain in opposition to His programme and to contend for the allegiance of the souls of men. We get a clear view of his activities in the story of our Lord's temptation. Here the main features of his character are delineated for us: (*a*) independence of the will of God, (*b*) desire for personal power, (*c*) consistent opposition to the plan of God which culminated in the Cross (Matt. iv, 1-11; cf. also our Lord's reply to Peter in Matt. xvi, 21-23). Our Lord connects physical illness with his activity, not only in the case of definite demon-possession (e.g. Matt. xii, 22-26), but also in what we should describe as a purely organic disease (Luke xiii, 11, 16). In the book of Job the same power is assigned to him, and few Christians who have been through the deep waters of temptation and suffering will dispute the words of St. Paul in Eph. vi, 12, where he describes the personal Satanic opposition to the Christian warrior. Above all, Satan desires power over the souls of men (e.g. Luke xxii, 31; 2 Tim. ii, 26), which the present state of the world shows that he is well able to obtain and exercise.

To the suggestion that she should act in independence of God's known will—a suggestion that we have seen to be entirely in keeping with the character of Satan as shown us in the New Testament—Eve as a free moral agent gave her fatal assent. She used her God-given independent will to foster her own ends instead of those of her Creator. Thus the fundamental sin of Satan became the fundamental sin of man. In the language of theology, man *fell*. From that day to this man has of himself acted in independence of God. Pride and self-seeking have been the mainspring of his actions. But the consequences were greater even than this. "In the day that thou eatest thereof thou shalt surely die." God's words were no idle threat. Their assertion of independence meant a life of independence; a life independent of Him in whom all live and move and have their being; a life that was but a living death. "Man, being in honour and abiding not, is made like unto the beasts that perish" (Ps. xlix, 12). The natural tendency of his body to decay now runs its uninterrupted course; death is his end, and death his present state. The spiritual world in which he was made to live slips from his grasp; shamed, he puts a tree between himself and his Creator, and the beauty of his body, now prostituted to his rebellious will, he seeks to hide with its leaves. He is spiritually dead; no other word is adequate to describe the contrast with his former state. Even the animal creation suffers, having lost its leader, the day of whose restoration it eagerly awaits (Rom. viii, 19-21).

At this point we must pause for a moment in order to touch on a question which insistently arises in our minds, especially in days of widespread suffering: if God is indeed an all-powerful and all-loving Creator, why did He allow such an event to take place in His universe, and such a being as Satan to continue to exist? Logically we ought to ask also why He allows such a being as fallen man to continue to exist, but this question does not seem to trouble the objectors to the Christian view of God and evil! To state this logical corollary of our earlier question is half-way to answering it. God has given man—and Satan—an inalienable creaturely existence (we need not here discuss whether this is necessarily everlasting; it is sufficient that man at any rate has the power of continually propagating his kind). To terminate this existence at the first act of rebellion in Satan and then in man would be to admit failure in their original creation. Further, there is the glorious possibility that some at least of mankind may attain by redemption a fuller and richer life than was Adam's in innocence, and we are encouraged by Scripture to regard this as the culminating act of the whole drama of creation. If the characters of that drama are to be real, and not mere puppets, they must be free to play their parts as they have chosen. If God has desired a world in which free creatures may worship Him, it must be a world in which free creatures may rebel against Him, or their freedom is no freedom at all. The Bible goes further and implies in more than one passage that the Fall has been included in the plan of God because the full glory of God's redemptive love and His power to preserve and deliver His own can be adequately shown only if the necessary antithesis of rebellion, opposition and wrath is allowed to exist also. See Rom. ix, 19-24; 1 Pet. ii, 4-10; Prov. xvi, 4. There is mystery here, and we cannot penetrate it further. Christian faith does not solve the problem of evil for the inquiring intellect; it resolves it for the individual

Christian in the liberating offer of redemption, and for the universal creation in the coming of the Reign of God.

The universe being planned on a consistent basis, man reaps the consequences of his own actions. God does not yet cause wars to cease in all the world, or remove the scourge of disease and famine. If man had continued to learn from God and to depend on Him, thereby experiencing the control of his body and of nature which he was intended to exercise, these things need not have been. Yet the careful student of nature knows of many things long before the days of man which seem to him inconsistent with belief in the goodness of the Creator. In face of this we can only say here that appearances are often deceptive, but that if some of these things are unquestionably evil, we may perhaps associate them with Satanic activities of which Scripture has little to tell us. However, it is idle to speculate in such matters, and it is not relevant to Christian faith.

Let us then return to fallen man, for it is of small consequence to treat the dry-rot in the house if we ourselves are suffering from smallpox. And, indeed, our trouble can be likened to a disease. The most serious consequence of the fall of Adam is an infection of our human nature which will need our most careful and honest consideration.

We have seen that men as we find them now, we ourselves in fact, are capable of the better and achieve the worse. We inquired into the origin of this state of affairs, and we found in the book of Genesis the story of the entry of sin into human life. Outside evil influences found a response in the inner nature of man. These devilish forces are still with us, and to them we still at times respond. In fact, we reiterate in our own lives the story of Adam and Eve. But there is one very important and crucial difference. *We begin where Adam left off.* Adam began in innocence, in perfect moral equipoise, free to choose good or evil. The evil choice once made, he knew himself for what he was—a rebel; and he fled his Maker. The way down into sin was easy: lies and unmanly excuses followed upon disobedience; the way back to God was hard— nay, impossible except God Himself take the initiative in

restoring it. This is where we begin. At one blow the vital link between man's spirit and God is severed, and the consequences of that severance devolve upon the whole race. There is a spiritual specific difference between fallen and unfallen human nature, so that now in the smallest infant disobedience is pleasurable, and substantiates the truth of David's words: "Behold, I was shapen in iniquity, and in sin did my mother conceive me" (Ps. li, 5). We do not, of course, imply that this warped nature, this proneness to evil, resides in us simply because we have a human body: the epitaph:

> "Here lies that part of Thomas Wood
> Which kept his soul from doing good,"

is sheer paganism, and has no place in Christ's teaching. Our body has sinful tendencies because we who live in it are sinful, and not vice versa. It is the spiritual nature which we derive from our parents, not that perfect little body which is its vehicle, that carries the infection.

This doctrine of original sin is not popular today; in fact, I do not know when it has ever been. But it is forced upon us on all quarters; as has been well said, if we will not take it from Augustine, we shall have to take it from Freud! No other explanation is adequate to explain the facts. It does not mean we are all born criminals; it means simply that from our earliest conscious days we put ourselves in the centre of our thinking, and not God. And that is sin. Our true centre is the worship of our Maker; and to put self in that central place is to be eccentric, unbalanced, sinful. Pride is the core of all our trouble, just as the badly-centred shaft wears out both itself and its bearings.

But if we are born like this, and in the nature of the case we cannot help ourselves, surely we are not responsible for it? Why call it sin, with its moral stigma, when it is only our unavoidable bias? This is a popular attempt to turn the edge of the blade that wounds our pride. But a little reflection should convince us that it cannot stand.

In the first place, our self-centred state in which we are born is an imperfection in God's world which must affront

His holy desire for an ordered creation. We are out of place, a jarring note in the symphony of praise to the Creator which He cannot let pass uncorrected.

> " . . . Disproportioned sin
> Jarred against nature's chime, and with harsh din
> Broke the fair music that all creatures made
> To their great Lord."
>
> MILTON, *At a Solemn Music.*

No musician who claims to be an artist can tolerate a false note in the production of a composer's work; to do so would be to betray the master's inspiration, and such an error, even if innocently made, will rightly receive blame. We are verily guilty for our sinful state, and it deserves God's wrath and condemnation. But, as Dr. Griffith Thomas says in his exposition of the Church of England Article in which these words occur[1], this is very different from saying that every case of inborn sinfulness actually receives the divine judgment. Between our sin and God's judgment lies the redemptive work of Christ, and the writer most certainly believes that no infant is condemned for sin which has never been translated into conscious responsible acts of will, but that the work of Christ avails for him without his conscious acceptance of it.

In the second place, we do express this innate proneness to sin in deliberate acts for which our conscience rightly castigates us. We know we ought to act otherwise—in fact, we know that at other times we have ourselves acted otherwise and that certainly there exist men who in similar circumstances have done right where we have failed. We say we have not done our best, thereby admitting that the best is 'ours', certainly as regards responsibility, if not as regards possibility of attainment. We may to ourselves excuse a child many things by saying he is not old enough to know better, but we are right to upbraid him for them and to teach him to overcome them; indeed, he himself will with increasing understanding pass increasing censure on himself. We are not machines, forced to sin, and wrong is no less reprehensible because we are prone to it.

[1] Griffith Thomas, *Principles of Theology*, p. 167 (Longmans).

Thirdly, our own human standards of justice imply responsibility. No judge would acquit a convicted thief because he pleaded his innate tendency to steal. Every time we blame another person for his conduct we assume his moral accountability; and though we may excuse ourselves when others blame us, we only reveal more fully our own moral responsibility by our endeavours to suppress it. We disapprove of Adam's meanness in shifting the blame on to Eve, and try to do the same ourselves when conscience condemns us.

There is one more serious word. Everyone who reads this has had opportunity of knowing God's offer of redemption from this entail of sin through the death of Jesus Christ. We are answerable to God for our acceptance or our rejection of that offer, and to reject is the most terrible sin of which we can be guilty, the sin which will ultimately cause even the love of God to cease to move us and leave us to our own company in hell.

Sin, then, is a disease of our nature, an assertion of our independence of the laws of God, which shows itself in symptomatic actions which we call sins. They may or may not be criminal—wronging our neighbour, or vicious—wronging ourselves, but they are failures to respond to the laws of God, and therefore we call them by their right name—sins. This disease has infected every part of us, our thinking and reasoning, our desires and affections, our motives and will. For our personality is an integral unit, and what affects one department must affect all. Of course, we are not as rotten as we possibly can be—the phrase 'total depravity' which is sometimes used was never meant to imply that; rather it means that there is no part of us which is wholly subject to the law of God. Of ourselves we cannot reason correctly about spiritual things—our selfish bias is apt to lead us into all kinds of false conclusions; we cannot love God with all our heart and with all our strength; and we cannot put ourselves right. We are in desperate need of God's help. And the glory of the Christian message is just here, that God has come down to help us. He has provided a way out of our plight, a way by which we may return to Himself. More still, for even with the way plain before us we cannot of ourselves turn us about to walk in it, He creates in us the impulse of will which yields our distorted personalities into His remoulding hands and brings us again into that position where our selfish independent wills are bent into dependence on Him. This matchless theme we must now turn to consider.

CHAPTER V

GOD DELIVERS MAN

On the afternoon of the first Easter Sunday two men were returning from Jerusalem to their home in the country. They were talking together of the stirring events they had witnessed in the Holy City during the recent Feast. Like others before them, they had been awaiting the day when God would take upon Himself to deliver man and to redeem His people Israel, which to them was the first step in this deliverance. Something about the life and teaching of Jesus of Nazareth had convinced them that He was God's appointed deliverer, but two days ago He had met His death at the hands of the Jewish rulers. So fair a prospect had ended in stark tragedy. They were bitterly disappointed, and their faces betrayed the fact.

As they walked, a stranger met them and inquired why they were sad. They recounted the story once more, glad to have a sympathetic listener. But he seemed not in the least perturbed. On the contrary, he gently chided them for being surprised: this was the very way they ought to have expected deliverance to come. Their Law and their prophets had spoken of this very thing—the Cross was the way of deliverance. They grew interested and soon they found themselves at the end of the journey which familiarity had made monotonous. They invited the stranger in to supper. He took the part of host, saying grace and breaking bread. But what are those scars in his hands? With a glance at one another they look again at his face, and even as they look, He vanishes out of their sight. Joy comes welling up in their hearts, and with it the memory of their Master's words: "The Son of Man must suffer and be killed, and the third day be raised up" (Luke ix, 22; xxiv, 13-32).

From that day to this the Cross has been a mystery to men until they meet the Crucified for themselves. Yet God had prepared the way beforehand in many ways. Man's failure to understand is due to the effect of sin on his mind. We may illustrate by saying that fallen man is in the position of enemy-occupied territory. He belongs to God His Maker, but the government has been usurped by a traitor within, which the Bible calls 'the flesh', which has accepted Satan's 'protection' and allowed his forces right of entry. Satan's first act has been to withhold reliable information of the outside spiritual world. Man has been left to grope in the dark, and the devil keeps him as far as possible in ignorance of God, and of his own enslavement. "The god of this world hath blinded the minds of the unbelieving, that the light of the gospel of the glory of Christ, who is the image of God, should not dawn upon them" (2 Cor. iv, 4, R.V.). Man imagines himself free until he sees the true freedom enjoyed by those whom God has liberated. Then he finds too late that he cannot deliver himself. The only way of deliverance, by yielding to God in Christ, is repellent to him.

It is clear, then, that God must take the initiative in the liberation of man, and in the revelation to man of the meaning of His own acts. The glorious message of the Christian gospel is that God has done so. The usurper has been conquered and the continued exercise of his power is mere bluff. As we read in Hebrews ii, 14, 15 (R.V.), Christ became man "that through death He might bring to nought him that had the power of death, that is, the devil; and might deliver all them who through fear of death were all their lifetime subject to bondage". But the way of deliverance will seem strange to us unless we take care to study the explanation which God gave in preparation for the event. This revelation was given to the Jews in the Old Testament to prepare them to receive the meaning of the Incarnation, Death and Resurrection of Jesus Christ, and to pass on their understanding to the world. Let us review it in detail.

At the first moment of defeat in the Garden there came from the lips of the Almighty the primal promise of deliverance: "Her seed," He said to the serpent, "shall bruise thy head, and thou shalt bruise his heel" (Gen. iii, 15). As time

43

went on this message was amplified in two ways: the person of the deliverer was delineated with increasing clearness, and the way of deliverance by sacrifice was illustrated and foreshadowed in ritual and prophecy. The Deliverer was to be a prophet like unto Moses (Deut. xviii, 18), a priest after the order of Melchizedek (Ps. cx, 4), a king of the house of David (Ps. lxxxix, 3, 4), a branch of the stock of Jesse (Isa. xi, 1), a servant of God who shall reign through suffering (Isa. lii, 13-liii, 12). He will be born in Bethlehem (Mic. v, 2), show His glory in Galilee (Isa. ix, 1-7), enter Jerusalem in triumph upon the peaceful ass (Zech. ix, 9), and there exercise His reign (Ps. ii, 6), which shall be universal and everlasting.

Alongside of this, God also revealed that His chosen deliverer would be a sin-offering (Isa. liii, 4-6, 10) and all that that implied. This fact is hinted at in some of these very passages, as well as in many others, but it was never fully understood by the Jews. From earliest times man was taught to approach God by sacrifice, and yet to realize that sacrifice of animals could never in itself atone for sin. The words of Abraham in Genesis xxii, 8, "God will provide Himself the lamb for a burnt-offering", meant more than, perhaps, Abraham understood at the time, but their full meaning was only seen when John the Baptist could stand and say: "Behold the Lamb of God which taketh away the sin of the world" (John i, 29).

God revealed to the children of Israel that sacrifice meant at least two primary things: the substitution of the death of an animal for that of the offerer as the just consequence of his sin—a substitution which was, of course, in no sense adequate, but was symbolic and pointed forward to the true Sacrifice for the sin of the world; and secondly, the entire devotion of the offerer to the will of God as shown in the complete consumption of the burnt-offering on the altar.

Every faithful Israelite who broke the law of God and brought his sacrifice thereby confessed that his own life was forfeit for his sin. But in its place he offered his victim's life, and by shedding its blood he emphasized the pouring out of that life to God: "For it is the blood that maketh atonement by reason of the life" (Lev. xvii, 11). Finally, he devoted his life to God as he offered his burnt-offering.

Those with most intimate knowledge of the mind of God realized the emptiness of ritual acts[1] which could not in themselves take away sin; but only in the New Testament, and especially in the great Epistle to the Hebrews (which should be the constant study of every Christian who would understand his Old Testament), do we fully learn the meaning and the imagery of these anticipatory rites.

Finally, God prepared for the day of liberation by convincing the oppressed of their bondage. Satan not only endeavours to conceal from man God's love to him, but also his own state of powerlessness; man, a slave to his passions and his enemy, believes himself to be free. God must therefore bring home to him his true condition. This He does by making very clear to him the moral law, the law of his being, his true charter of liberty. Through the promptings of conscience, through the clear revelation to Moses on Sinai, through the persistent call of the prophets to righteousness and holy living, man, if he is honest, learns his utter inability to serve God as He requires. The law is his schoolmaster[2] to bring him to Christ (Gal. iii, 24).

At length, and in the fulness of time, when some at least of Israel had learnt and understood these lessons, and the written records were complete for those who came after to read, God sent forth His Son, born of a woman (Gal. iv, 4), and that incursion of God into the realm of man took place which we know as the Incarnation of our Lord and Saviour Jesus Christ.

We are left in no doubt as to why He came. He came to redeem (Gal. iv, 5), to seek and to save the lost (Luke xix, 10), to give His life a ransom for many (Mark x, 45), to save His people from their sins (Matt. i, 21). The announcement is plain for all to hear: the plan for man's liberation is being put

[1] *See* e.g. Pss. xl, 6-8, li, 16-19; Isa. i, 11-18; Mic. vi, 6-8.
[2] The Greek word used here (παιδαγωγός) means the slave whose duty it was to conduct the young son of the house to school, carrying his books, etc. Once arrived, we must submit to our Teacher, to find that He treats us as sons.

45

into effect—the Father has sent the Son to be the Saviour of the world (1 John iv, 14). This plan culminates in the Cross; here must the Son of Man be lifted up, that the work which He was sent to do may be finished. The whole ministry of Jesus Christ moves inevitably to this climax, and the portion of the Gospel story devoted to the last week of our Lord's life is out of all proportion to the rest. In short, as we read our New Testament we are made to feel that here, on the hill of Calvary, is the centre of gravity of the Christian message, the focal point of the light that has gleamed through the pages of prophecy and now shines out into all the world. The most vital question then that we can ask is: "What is the meaning of this event for Christianity, for *me?*" The event has given a word to our language, for it is in the fullest sense *crucial*, a crisis which judges men.

We are bound to confess at the outset that the meaning transcends all our understanding. Not only would the whole world not suffice to contain all the books that might be written of it (John xxi, 25), but human thought and language cannot adequately compass its scope. We are forced to describe it in human terms, by human analogies, and using human illustrations, and all such are only partial views of God's eternal truth. We shall take three such views, but not so as to pretend that they comprise the whole. The Cross of our Lord Jesus Christ, then, demonstrates the love of God, satisfies the holiness of God, and in the union of these two provides the only perfect sacrifice for the sin of man.

First, then, the Cross demonstrates the love of God. This must be the first action of God in liberation. He must demonstrate to man, whom Satan has tried to keep in ignorance of Him and His character, that He still loves His creature and longs to save him from his bondage. He must prove beyond a doubt, to continue our original metaphor, that His invading forces are sent to reunite, to reintegrate man's personality, and to win him back to his true loyalty. He comes as friend, not foe; to be loved, not dreaded. The Cross is a place of wooing. "In this was manifested the love of God toward us, because that God sent His only-begotten Son into the world" (1 John iv, 9). Coming at the close of a life spent in service drawn out by compassion for the multitudes, the Cross showed the utmost outpouring of the love of God for men; "having loved His own," John says of his Master, "He loved them unto the end" (John xiii, 1). To the Roman criminal's gibbet He would go (and even then pray for those who nailed Him there), because His deeds of mercy excited the envy of the religious leaders, and because He refused to fight for an earthly kingdom which the nationalism of His day demanded. No doubt they would have been well satisfied had He used His undoubted power to free them from Rome; but He was concerned with a deeper evil and one that affected the common people more intimately—the sin of the human heart and the physical suffering so often associated with it. And so He proved His love for men, though it cost Him Calvary.

But if that were all, if His death were but a noble and moving example of martyrdom, He would have done no more than countless others have done. There is no liberating power here; only a glimpse of freedom unattained. Not only did He show God's love for sinners, He also showed God's hatred of sin. On the Cross He was not only the victim of man's sin, He voluntarily took it upon Himself. He bare our sins in His own body on the tree, says St. Peter (1 Pet. ii, 24). God there showed to man that sin brings tragedy and punishment in its train, for God is holy and God must punish sin. So while man's sin brought on himself the tragedy of man's rejection and murder of his Saviour, God at that moment was in Christ bearing man's sin—its guilt and penalty—(2 Cor. v, 19) upon Himself. Here is the holy wrath of God against sin, visited upon Jesus Christ, God's incarnate Self, instead of upon man, the guilty offender. As He there bore the guilt of sin, in some mysterious way the Father's face was turned from Him, so that He must cry out: "My God, My God, why hast Thou forsaken me?" before He can say: "It is finished." This is not to say that Jesus offered Himself to appease an angry Deity

47

who would otherwise have broken out in dire punishment of man. Such a thought is sub-Christian. The Cross is God's work; God has planned it from His heart of love, and God here takes the initiative in redeeming man. But God is not only love, He is holiness; His character is justice, and the world He has made is a moral world where sin receives punishment; hence, to forgive sin lightly, glibly and indulgently is to contradict Himself and to throw a morally ordered world into confusion. If we may speak in human terms, however much God's love prompts Him to restore fallen man to favour, God's holiness prompts Him to punish man's persistent rebellion. There is no conflict in God, for God is One, and in Him love and holiness are perfectly united. For the full meaning of this we must look again to the Cross, where "mercy and truth are met together: righteousness and peace have kissed each other" (Ps. lxxxv, 10).[1]

The message of the Cross is that God is both just and the justifier of the ungodly, and this because the Holy Sufferer is both God and Man. Here our third view will cast some light. The hill of Calvary has many aspects. From its summit all is clear, but on its summit there is a Cross and One alone hangs there, the Man Jesus Christ, the only mediator between God and man (1 Tim. ii, 5). We can but humbly survey the many sides of the hill; if from one side its ravines seem obscure and forbidding, from another we may discern its topography more clearly.

Let us look then at the event in the light of those sacrifices which God gave to man to prepare his mind to receive the truth concerning His Son. We have seen that those sacrifices had two main significations—substitution of an innocent victim for the guilty offender, and devotion of the life of the victim as a pledge to God. To punish a substitute is not just unless the substitute is the judge, the embodiment of the broken law; to devote another life to God is valueless unless the offerer has some personal interest in the victim and is identified with him in spirit. Unless, then, Christ is both

[1] See further Appendix III on the Terminology of Atonement.

man and God the Cross is neither just nor efficacious. But that is exactly what He is. As God He takes upon Himself the death penalty for the broken law; as Man He yields to God the perfect sinless life of obedience which no man before or since has been able to do. He is both Priest and Victim, the only full, perfect and sufficient sacrifice, oblation and satisfaction for the sins of the whole world.

The pious Israelite who brought his sin-offering laid his hand on the head of the victim, confessing his sin. If I by faith so link myself with my Saviour, I may find in Him my sin-bearer and my substitute, and experience the pardon of God for all my guilt.

> Not all the blood of beasts
> On Jewish altars slain
> Could give the guilty conscience peace,
> Or wash away its stain.
>
> But Christ, the Heavenly Lamb,
> Takes all our sins away;
> A sacrifice of nobler Name
> And richer blood than they.
>
> My faith would lay her hand
> On that dear head of Thine,
> Where like a penitent I stand
> And there confess my sin.
>
> My soul looks back to see
> The burden Thou didst bear
> When hanging on the accursed tree,
> And knows her guilt was there.

Plainly, then, the Cross clears the way for man's forgiveness, but how does it effect man's liberation? By itself it did not. Yet though, in the words of Peter's magnificent paradox, men killed the Prince of Life (Acts iii, 15), through death God conquered him that had the power of death (Heb. ii, 14). The death of Calvary was the gateway to Resurrection.

The Resurrection on the third morning is inseparable from

the death of our Lord on the Cross. It proves the reality of the victory of Calvary, turns tragedy into triumph, and perplexity into deliverance and praise. It is always described in the New Testament as God's act; it is the seal of His acceptance of the sacrifice of His Son, the triumph of His holiness over the foul miasma of the realm of Satan—"Thou wilt not . . . suffer Thy Holy One to see corruption" (Ps. xvi, 10). Death, the last stronghold of Satan's power, is conquered and the public subjugation of the enemy and deceiver is now only a matter of time. If the sacrifice of Calvary delivers me from sin's guilt and penalty, the Resurrection gives me a living Saviour in whose name I can claim my freedom and who will Himself bring me victory over the enemies of my soul.

CHAPTER VI

GOD REDEEMS ME

WE have now sketched, albeit very inadequately, the broad outline of God's plan to deliver man; but the all-important question remains: how is this plan to be applied in detail to the liberation of any particular person—to be precise, of *me?* How does God bring home and apply to me the result of these great cosmic events in the spiritual world?

For answer we may begin with the words of the Lord Jesus on the night of His betrayal. As He gave the cup to His disciples He said: "This cup is the new covenant in my blood" (Luke xxii, 20). The word used would take His hearers back to Old Testament times, where God made a covenant with Israel whereby they were to be His people, obedient to His laws, and He would be their God, blessing them and their land with prosperity. Indeed, the very occasion on which these words were spoken was a commemoration of Israel's deliverance from Egypt, which had been accompanied by the sacrifice of the Passover lamb, and the sprinkling of its blood on the doors of their houses. Thus the first covenant was sealed "in blood", and with blood its first written embodiment was sprinkled (Exod. xxiv, 8; Heb. ix, 18-20, x, 29, xiii, 20). This covenant failed in a sense, because the people of Israel were powerless to keep their share in its terms, though it accomplished God's purpose, which was to prove to them that very powerlessness. Now Jesus Christ offers to men a new covenant "in *His* blood". God is prepared to enter into a new relationship with man in consequence of the work of Christ on the Cross. "Christ, our Passover, has been sacrificed" (1 Cor. v, 7). God has now invaded the realm of human life and He is going to overthrow the Satanic powers of evil. He is prepared to give freedom and status to all who will accept and meet His terms. Those who refuse must of necessity be involved in the overthrow.

Of course, it is true that God has always been ready to enter into a personal relationship with individuals. We have only to think of Abraham, of Moses, of David, of the long list of heroes of faith in Hebrews xi, to see that this is so. But this was in anticipation of the work of Christ, and it was never thrown open to the whole Gentile world. To some of the greatest of the Old Testament saints it was revealed in detail that there would be a new covenant based on forgiveness, which would bring with it the power to carry it out. Jeremiah, in a notable passage, which is also quoted in the New Testament (Jer. xxxi, 31-34, Heb. viii, 8-12), describes this new covenant which God would make with Israel. But now in Christ the new relationship is offered freely to all.

This new relationship is described in the New Testament by three similes: it is like the relationship of a son to his father, of a slave to his master, and of a wife to her husband.

First, then, we are the sons of God our Father (John i, 12; Rom. viii, 14-17; 1 John iii, 1, 2). This involves many things. To begin with, on the negative side, Christians do not believe in the universal fatherhood of God except in a very limited sense, exemplified in Mal. ii, 10, and Acts xvii, 28, where we are called His offspring, in that we are His creatures. To be children of God is a privilege reserved for those who enter voluntarily into this relationship—who submit themselves to being 'reborn' into God's family. It means a new life, the very life of God, implanted in our souls; a new privilege as members of the great family of God; and a new inheritance into which we enter more and more fully and of which our present experience is but the paid deposit, an inheritance which is nothing less than the whole of God's universe. To think of God's Fatherhood as meaning that He is like an indulgent parent who responds to every whim of His children and desires their uninstructed sentimental affection is a travesty of the truth, which emasculates the whole conception of Christian sonship and replaces the God and Father of our Lord Jesus Christ by a benevolent 'Grandfather-in-heaven'.

Lest we should slip into this lethargic conception the New Testament writers prefer to speak of themselves as the slaves of Christ and of Him as their Master and Owner. We are His purchased possessions, bought at the cost of His own blood (Acts xx, 28; 1 Cor. vi, 19, 20). A slave belongs entirely to his master, and he is expected to give him implicit obedience. If we enlist in the forces of liberation our position is indeed one of privilege, but it is also one of discipline. We are pledged to obey our Captain's orders. Freedom is not anarchy, and man is not created to be utterly independent. He is a little lower than the angels, although he is made to have dominion (Ps. viii, 5, 6). The spiritual world is above him, and the powers of evil and of good contend for his soul. If he is freed from the evil, he must serve the good—there is no neutrality. In a certain Central African tribe there are two classes of slave: the casual worker who takes a holiday just when he likes and enjoys protection of his person only so long as he is engaged in his chief's service; and the lifelong slave who is bound at all times to answer his chief's call. For him all his master's resources are always available; if he or any of his family suffer wrong, he may claim the help of his chief, and he is bound to give it to the utmost of his capacity. The Christian's relation to his Lord is intended to be of the second kind.

The third aspect of the covenant-relationship concerns the participators in the covenant as a whole. It is what we call a *corporate* relationship, for it concerns them as a single body, related to Christ as a wife to her husband. The emphasis here is on the intimacy of our connection with God, and on the delight which we should find in fellowship with Him. This will be more clearly seen in Chapter VIII, when we shall see what Christ means by His Church, but it cannot be omitted here. We are called to be friends of God, not merely His slaves. A slave does not know much of his master's business; the general does not confide his plans to the private soldier; but Jesus calls us His friends and makes His Church His earthly bride (John xv, 15; Eph. v, 25-30).

God, then, offers to individuals a pardon for their rebellion, without which they could expect only well-deserved punishment for their opposition, and also a complete reinstatement made possible by the death of His Son, which He calls the new covenant in His blood. This is the marvellous and gracious offer which, we should expect, would meet with universal acceptance.

But does it? For answer we have only to look at our own experience. My reason warped, my will-power weakened by Satan's long-continued lying propaganda, I will not, and so long as I will not, I cannot, respond to His offer. God will not force it upon me—He wants volunteers, not conscripts—but He can and does make me willing to accept it. It is impossible to separate what God does and what I do in the act of acceptance. Certainly, it is God's offer, and it is God who inclines my will to take it. My part is called faith, and that is God's gift to me! (Eph. ii, 8). So it all depends on God, and yet in a sense it all depends on me! Multitudes of Christians have wrestled with this paradox and left it unresolved. The facts of experience and of revelation are plain enough; the offer is a perfectly fair one and it is open to us to take it or leave it: some accept it, some do not; those who accept it soon realize that it was only the grace of God that made them do so; those who reject it recognize their full responsibility for rejection and usually do so on quite other grounds than their supposed inability to accept. In fact, to know oneself unable to accept God's offer is a sure sign of the working of God's grace in the heart. No true seeker will be left unsatisfied, but it is a terrible thing to harden the heart against the grace of God.

Man's side of this event we may call 'conversion'; God's side is usually spoken of as 'regeneration'—perhaps a frightening term to those without a classical upbringing. I am afraid that there is no real alternative for it; it is necessary to be precise, and all precise language if it is not intolerably prolix requires technical terms. Regeneration means "bringing to birth again"—implanting a new life.

Conversion and regeneration are not separate successive events, nor even contemporaneous processes: they are the same thing. Like the obverse and reverse of a coin, one is seen from below, from the viewpoint of man's experience, the other from God's side, from above. The lower side shows the value and meaning of the event for man; the upper side bears the royal image and imprint and stamps it as the work of God.

Conversion is in two parts: looking back and looking forward. We look back on our past rebellion with regret and loathing. We begin to appreciate a little of God's view of the situation, and we *repent*. We experience a change of mind about ourselves—for this is the root meaning of the N.T. word for repentance. We see ourselves as mean and selfish and ugly, ridiculous in our pride, contemptible in our conceit. We realize that this is *sin*, an affront in the face of God, and that Calvary is the measure of its cost. It is not so much that we have done this and that, as that we are creatures who can do that sort of thing and enjoy it. We turn away from our past selves in horror—and we find ourselves facing our Saviour. In fact, we *convert*, or more truly, as we recognize the working of God's Spirit, we *are converted*. We turn to God, and find Him not hounding us in His wrath, but extending to us His pardon. From the printed page or the living voice of His witness we hear the gracious offer: "Seek ye the Lord while He may be found, call ye upon Him while He is near: let the wicked forsake his way and the unrighteous man his thoughts: and let him return unto the Lord, and He will have mercy upon him; and to our God, for He will abundantly pardon" (Isa. lv, 6-7). We see ourselves as the rebels for whom Christ died; He was wounded, we say, for our transgressions, and we appropriate His sacrifice for ourselves: with His stripes we are healed (Isa. liii, 5). We believe it was for us He hung and suffered there; therefore we commit ourselves and our cause to our Saviour. For the first time we come to God as a son to a father, as a slave to his master. As a woman plights her troth to a man, so we are pledged to Christ. We have entered upon the new relationship.

Regeneration similarly is twofold: God gives us pardon for the past, and life for the future. In the first place we are *justified*. This means more than mere acquittal, but at the same time it does not mean we become immediately perfect— we need hardly suppose that Christians are asked to believe anything so opposed to experience—faith is not persuading oneself to believe what is not true! God's forgiveness is not only a negative thing, forgetting our past misdeeds; we are given a definite status which we do not deserve, because we are now linked in God's reckoning with Christ. He accepts responsibility for us, and because of what He is we receive a new dignity. If a man of noble character and reputation wins the love and devotion of a poor, sinful woman and, freely forgiving her past, makes her his honourable wife, he gives her a dignity and status which she could never herself have achieved. She is accepted socially because of her husband's character; she can transact business in her husband's name; she is reckoned to be other than she was. Further, if she is really devoted to her husband she will very soon begin to *be* other than she was. No one imagines she will immediately become a model character, but a process has been set on foot which, with her willing co-operation, will do much to change her.

This gives us some idea of what justification means. St. Paul tells us that our sin is imputed to Christ, so that He bore its punishment; while God's righteousness is imputed to us, justifying us through faith in Christ.[1] To modern minds this sounds like a legal fiction, but it is a vital fact of experience resulting from our spiritual union with Christ. We can in very truth look back to Calvary and see our sins there receiving their due reward; while we can and may stand humbly but boldly in God's presence because the presence of His Spirit in our hearts gives us the right and the desire to call Him Father (Rom. viii, 15).

This is the second aspect of regeneration. We are reinstated because the very life of God is given to us. Just as in the first creation the breath of God brought life to man, so now man is made again by the Spirit of God. There is, in fact, a new creation (2 Cor. v, 17). God makes anew the spiritual part of man, long dulled by sin and atrophied by disuse, by the direct working of the Holy Spirit, the person of the Godhead who is the agent in carrying out God's programme as it relates

[1] *See* Rom. iii, 21-26, iv, 4-8; 2 Cor. v, 21; Phil. iii 9.

to the spirit of man. The late Bishop Taylor Smith used to illustrate this in the following way: we are, he said, like a candle; the wax is our body, the wick our mental powers, and the flame our spiritual life. We were made for spiritual fellowship with God, just as the candle is made to give light. Flame results from the union of the products of wax and wick with the air, but it must first be ignited. There is no more subtle error than that which talks of the divine spark within us which only needs fanning to burst into flame. The New Testament tells us unequivocally that we are dead, and that the spark of life must come to us from outside. We have the materials for spiritual life, but life itself we have not; God must give it us, and this gift is a miracle of creative power (2 Cor. iv, 6).

This experience is the core of the Christian gospel. It has been the theme of Christian song and thanksgiving from apostolic days down to today. The New Testament describes it with a bewildering variety of language. We are forgiven, cleansed, justified by the grace of God; we receive Christ, are baptized of His Spirit, made sons of the Father; we are converted, born again, transferred from the kingdom of Satan into the kingdom of Heaven.

Two questions must be answered before we leave this subject: (a) is it a sudden experience? and (b) is it a lasting experience?

First, is it a sudden experience? In a way, from God's point of view we might say there must be a time when God sees us as rebels, and a time when He makes us His sons. We cannot be neutral, and there is no half-way house, so that we might expect that the crucial miracle must be instantaneous. But God, we reflect, is not bound by time as we are, and we are not bound to limit and classify His actions in this way. Time is a matter of our experience, and certainly in our experience conversion may or may not be sudden. St. Paul yielded to Christ in a flash on the road to Damascus—but when was the miracle wrought in St. Peter's heart? Normally, for an adult ignorant of the gospel and confirmed in rebellion, conversion would seem to be sudden and often dramatic, though preceded by a period of increasing dissatisfaction and conviction of sin, which may be a long one; while for a child of Christian parents, nurtured in the fear of the Lord and receiving the sincere milk of the Word, there is, perhaps, more often a growing realization of the truth and appropriation of the gifts of God. Of one thing we must be very clear—we do not grow into spiritual life of our own accord. God works the miracle in us as we yield to Him; we are not Christians because our parents were or because we have been brought up to know the facts: we must consciously and voluntarily close with God's offer.

Secondly, is it a lasting experience? Is it not rather presumptuous to say that I am saved—that I know I have eternal life? Well, it is always presumptuous to *say* things unless they are borne out by the evidence of our lives; if we say these things there are certain differences which ought to be appearing in our lives which will substantiate our words. They will be found in St. John's first Epistle. Further, there are strong warnings in the New Testament (e.g. Heb. vi, 4-8, x, 26-31) against wilful sin, which suggest the possibility of a counterfeit experience. But this Epistle referred to was expressly written that we might know that we have eternal life (1 John v, 13), so evidently God intends us to be certain about it. On what is our assurance based? Primarily on the promises of God. The gifts and calling of God are without repentance (Rom. xi, 29). God promises to receive us, to give us eternal life, to make us His sons. No one, He says, can pluck us out of the Father's hand (John x, 29). A story is told of an aged Christian lady who quoted this verse to a sceptic who was trying to shake her faith. "But suppose," said he, "that God lets you slip through His fingers." "He can't," was the triumphant reply, "I'm one of the fingers!" Our union with God is organic and indissoluble. Further, the deposit of our inheritance has been paid (Eph. i, 13, 14) in the person of the Spirit of God Himself; He is the priceless guarantee of all that God has promised us, and He will bring us the conscious realization of the fact that we are the sons of God (Rom. viii, 16). God will not let us go. Our faith may flicker, our grip weaken, our zeal abate, but God will never be content with us until we attain the standard He has set for us. If we had to maintain the ardour of our first devotion we should all have given up long ago, but we have put our lives into the mighty hands of God and He will not rest till we are other than we are.

> Because the sinless Saviour died,
>   My sinful soul is counted free;
> For God, the Just, is satisfied
>   To look on Him and pardon me.
> One with Himself, I cannot die;
>   My soul is purchased with His blood;
> My life is hid with Christ on high,
>   With Christ, my Saviour and my God.

SUMMARY OF SECTION II

I. MAN

(1) *Innocence*. Man's personality was originally made in the image of God, so that he enjoyed fellowship with God and exercised authority over himself and the rest of creation.

(2) *The Fall*. Through a specific act of self-assertive rebellion early in his history, man has forfeited his authority and broken his fellowship with his Creator, thereby experiencing physical and spiritual death.

(3) *Sin*. As a natural consequence of this event the human race is now incapable of restoring the situation on its own initiative, and no department of human personality has remained unaffected.

(4) *Guilt*. Every man born into the world is prone to sin, and though his conscience approves the better, he is guilty of choosing the worse. For this deliberate choice he deserves the judgment of God.

II. REDEMPTION—GOD'S PART

(1) *Preparation*. God prepared man for the coming of Christ by giving the law to convince him of his failure: by the rite of sacrifice: and by the teaching of the prophets.

(2) *Incarnation*. God became man in the fulness of time, in the person of Jesus Christ.

(3) *Atonement*. The Cross of Christ demonstrates the love of God, satisfies the holiness of God, and is the only perfect substitutionary sacrifice for the repentant sinner.

(4) *Resurrection*. In raising Christ from the dead, the Father showed His acceptance of the Sacrifice, His victory over death, and His triumph over the forces of evil.

III. Redemption—Man's Part

(1) *Regeneration.* To the repentant and believing sinner God offers a new life through the entrance of the Holy Spirit.

(2) *Justification.* Those who accept this are forgiven and reinstated; God undertakes to perfect the work He has begun.

(3) *The New Covenant.* Christians are made sons of God, servants of Christ; they enjoy His friendship and form His earthly Bride.

GOD'S PLAN IN ACTION

CHAPTER VII

THE LIFE-GIVING SPIRIT

MANY people, if they think of God at all, regard Him as a kind of vague influence like the air we breathe or the genial warmth of the sun. Stained-glass windows have a peculiar focusing effect on this influence, so that beautiful churches become highly charged with it, but it remains completely impersonal and in no way to be reckoned with in the mundane transactions of life. The disciples of Christ, steeped in the thought and language of the Old Testament, had no such conception of God. To them the language of the twenty-ninth psalm would seem more appropriate: "The voice of the Lord is powerful; the voice of the Lord breaketh the cedars; the voice of the Lord cleaveth the flames of fire; the voice of the Lord shaketh the wilderness" (R.V.). The Spirit of God often means no more to us than a general benevolence, a desire to love our neighbour as ourselves; to them He was the One who inspired the mighty deeds of a Gideon and transported the prophets to the scenes of their majestic visions of God.

Thus prepared by the experiences of their nation, they recognized immediately the significance of the event which came to answer and interrupt their prayers on the day of Pentecost—the rushing wind and the tongues of fire were unmistakable. "This," said the now emboldened Peter, "is that which was spoken of by the prophet Joel." God is beginning to put into action the plan which the prophets foretold (Acts ii, 16).

What exactly does this event signify, and how ought we to think of it? God's invasion of human life in the Person of Jesus Christ is complete, culminating in the Resurrection of the One who had offered His own life on our behalf. Bearing the form of a man, He has moved out of the realm of immediate human experience, or as we say, "He ascended into Heaven". Yet God's work of liberation and restoration has only just started; why then remove the Commander at the critical hour? The answer given by Christ Himself to this question was twofold: He could more effectively consult the interests of His people if He were at the supreme headquarters of the Godhead—at the right hand of power of the Majesty on high; while He would then be with His people in a far more intimate way, by sending His Holy Spirit to be at the right hand of weakness, as we may put it—indwelling the personality of the individual Christian. Pentecost was the implementing of this promise.

The Holy Spirit is God in action: God as He works directly with human personalities. He is God in contact with me, confronting me, and if I am a Christian, living in me. He has personal dealings with me, so that I know that He is He, as Christ spoke of Him, not It, a vague influence from God. He is in this sense a person—not a separate being from the Father and the Son, but God in one of His three Persons.

This brings us face to face with the Christian doctrine of the Trinity, which must therefore claim our attention before we pass on to the distinctive work of the Holy Spirit. I suppose no doctrine has elicited more ridicule or given rise to more bewilderment than this. The battleground of Christian controversy for six centuries, it is strewn with battered terms and phrases which even now remind us of the tragic struggles which divided the Christian Church through her failure to understand the revelation of God. The difficulty arises because this is a specific doctrine about the nature of God as revealed by the facts of history and experience; and God, just because He is God, must in His entirety be unknowable to man. Man can find no language in which to describe what he sees of God, for there is nothing fully analogous in the whole range of human experience. Several partial analogies have been suggested; for example, the musical triad, or three-note chord, three entities in one complete whole; yet the three notes are distinct, and each does not by itself convey the whole. Whereas "He that hath seen Me hath seen the Father," says Jesus; and in promising the gift of the Spirit he can say: "We will come and make our abode with him" (John xiv, 9, 23). All human analogies fail similarly; either we can find three things which together form something quite different, like the musical chord, or else one thing which has three parts or aspects, such as Energy, Matter and Radiation, or St. Patrick's shamrock leaf. God does not *become* Christ, or *become* Holy Spirit; He is eternally three, yet eternally one.

Not only is there no adequate analogy, but difficulty arises in the very terms we have to use. We say that the Father, Son and Holy Spirit are three distinct Persons in One God, but it is practically impossible to give the word "person" as here used any content, except to say that it is the noun which stands to substantiate the adjective "three" in the above sentence. In the famous words of Augustine (*De Trin.*, v. 10): "Dictum est tamen, Tres Personæ, non ut illud diceretur sed ne taceretur"—I translate freely—"We say, Three Persons, not so as to make a definite statement, but to avoid saying nothing at all." Certainly no other word can be put in its place without being liable to misunderstanding. The Persons are not "modes" or "forms" of God; they are distinct. They are not "gods" or separate entities; there is one God and one divine Nature. They are not masks which the Godhead wears, as too close an adherence to the derivation of the word "person" might suggest; nor are they separate autonomous beings linked only by sharing in a common life, as we might deduce from the use of the word in English. "We may content ourselves with simply observing that to the New Testament there is but one only living and true God; but that to it Jesus Christ and the Holy Spirit are each God in the fullest sense of the term; and yet Father, Son and Spirit stand over against each other as I, and Thou, and He. When we have said these three things, then—that there is but one God, that the Father and the Son and the Spirit is each God, that the Father and the Son and the Spirit is each a distinct Person—

we have enunciated the doctrine of the Trinity in its completeness."[1]

The Mohammedan God is a lonely God. He has an eternal will, but He cannot love and is incapable of fellowship. The God and Father of our Lord Jesus Christ is Love; His nature is fellowship, and therefore there must be an eternal distinction between the three Persons. The Father is always the Father, loving the Son, planning for His world; the Son is always the Son, obeying the Father and delighting to do His will; the Spirit is always the Spirit, the agent of the Father in creation, brooding over the face of the waters, desiring the completion of the Father's purpose in the Kingdom of the Son (Gen. i, 2; Rev. xxii, 17). Once, at our Lord's baptism, we see each Person at His work; the Father's voice from heaven, sending the Spirit as a dove upon the Son as He emerges from the waters of obedience to His Father's will.

The doctrine of the Trinity cannot be explained, nor have we attempted to explain it. But it is to be believed in the light of Christian experience, as the early Church came to believe it. With all their zeal for Jewish monotheism they saw nothing inconsistent in ascribing Deity unequivocally to Jesus; and the Holy Spirit, whose power and acts were their daily experience, was soon joined with the Father and Son in their worship and in their formulæ of blessing, e.g. 2 Cor. xiii, 14.

When thus accepted by faith, the doctrine of the Holy Trinity is seen to be the fountain-head of the whole Christian Revelation. For through it we learn that the divided activities of the three Persons in Redemption reflect in human experience an eternal distinction between them. And it is in the work of Redemption that we see the fullest revelation that it is possible for us to see of the Triune God. The Father of those who believe in Jesus is the Eternal Father of the Son. The son born of the Virgin Mary is the Eternal Son of the Father. The love shown by the Father when He gave His Son on the Cross to be our Saviour: the love shown by the Son when through the Eternal Spirit He offered Himself without blemish unto God (Heb. ix, 14): this love is the Eternal Love of God

---

[1] Warfield, *Biblical Doctrines*, p. 147 (Oxford University Press).

in the fellowship of the three Persons. The mighty Spirit outpoured on the day of Pentecost is the Eternal Activity of the Godhead. God is One—one in will and character, nature and attributes: yet God is Three—three in person and fellowship, and in His relationship to man. The Father loved man and planned his salvation: the Son came, sent by the Father, to die on Calvary as the world's Redeemer; the Spirit, sent by the Father and by the Son now returned to His throne, completes the work in the life of the Christian.

The work of God the Holy Spirit is essentially creative. He is the agent who puts the Father's design into practice, God active in the affairs of men. We see Him at the outset moving in creative activity over the void; He guides the skilful hands of Bezaleel as he makes the greatest of God's foreshadowings of His coming Christ (Exod. xxxi, 2, 3); Zechariah sees Him as the motive power in the re-establishing of God's worship at Jerusalem (Zech. iv, 6). But there are two main directions in which His work is of present importance to us—His activity in the individual Christian and the corporate community of Christians which we call the Church; and His activity in that revelation of God to man which we call the Bible.

"I believe in the Holy Ghost, the Lord and Giver of Life," we say in the Creed which we call the Nicene Creed, though these clauses are later than Nicæa; and in these titles we sum up the relation of the Holy Spirit to the Christian. He is the Christian's Lord and the source of the Christian's life. This is the second part of the grand message which is the Christian faith: "I will not leave you orphans," says Christ as He tells His disciples of His coming death; "I will come to you" (John xiv, 18, margin); and by His Spirit He has come.

When a man first meets with and responds to the call of God he is no better than any of his fellow-men; all alike have marred by sin the image of God in which man was first created. When he is converted he receives the revolutionizing gift of forgiveness, an experience which can open the floodgates of gratitude and release into his life a new power. He finds a new centre for his devotion and service. But forgiveness is not enough, nor is it ever given alone. If God takes in

66

hand the battered coin of a human personality, He intends to remould it and to restore its defaced image—He which hath begun a good work in you will perform it. This work of restoration is the task of the Holy Spirit. It is an uphill task, running contrary to the forces of nature. Humanity and humanism are fine-sounding words, but "humanum est errare" is a truer estimate of human nature. God does not remove these tendencies from the Christian; He creates in him a spiritual life and gives him a power which will ultimately transform him. He never begins a work that He cannot finish. There is no life at all apart from the Spirit, the Life-giver, and no forgiveness apart from God-given repentance. And the Spirit is God active, unresting, untiring, refining the base metal from our lives until He sees His image mirrored in them.

There is much to be done. Sinful habits have to be rooted out, cowardice made bold, pride humbled to the dust. There is to be built up in us Christian virtue, likeness to our Master. Our thinking must be reoriented as we appreciate God's view of the world, our whole philosophy of life transformed. Every part of our being must share in the transforming process, so that Paul can speak of our putting off our old man and putting on the new (Col. iii, 9, 10), which is day by day being renewed into God's image. This is our sanctification. Potentially we are called saints from the moment of our entrance into life, for God sees us as we ideally shall be, wholly set apart for Him.[1] But we are far from holy, and so we are being sanctified. A saint is not one who has attained a certain degree of progress in holiness, as though he had passed with first-class honours in an examination and received the title at the hands of a college of ecclesiastics; if any Christian has advanced even a little way along the way of holiness, it is only to see more clearly the vastness of the distance which separates him from God's perfection, the depths of the depravity of his own heart. Our petty comparisons of ourselves with one another are utterly trivial beside the immeasurable failure of our best in the light of God's standard.

[1] The word ἅγιος, saint, is applied in the N.T. to *all* Christians. Its basic meaning is "set apart" or "devoted" to the service of God.

Most of us are afraid of holiness, even a little repelled by it. We think of a sort of unctuous piety, or an officious asceticism, like the boy who thought of God as looking round to see if anyone was enjoying himself and then stopping him. Needless to say, we have been misled by bad advertisements; holiness is the most attractive thing we can ever meet, though it has fire to burn up all that is mean in its presence. If we would see holiness, we have a fourfold picture given to us of its living embodiment, and a matchless sermon spoken by Him as to its principles and practice. Holiness is life to the full, wholeness of living, integrity of heart: our whole being united in doing the will of God for which we were made. This is the goal of God's work in us.

The Lord Jesus likens the work of the Holy Spirit in the Christian to a well of water springing up unto everlasting life (John iv, 14). The Christian is like an artesian well, which always flows because it is maintained by a permanent reservoir of water at a higher level than the outflow. At some places in England there are wells which at high tide are covered by the sea, yet they are never polluted by the salt water. The head of fresh water which produces the flow exerts a pressure which keeps the salt water out. So the Holy Spirit fills the Christian with satisfying water and makes him flow over in blessing to others though he may be constantly in touch with defiling things. The illustration, of course, is not perfect; the flow of the well is mechanical, but the holiness of the Christian involves his personality. It is sadly possible for either the inflow or the outflow to be blocked. Sooner or later the pressure of the Spirit will remove the obstruction, but it will be a costly process and it is better to keep the channel always clean.

There must be outflow—we are not to be made into beautiful placid characters like stagnant pools to be admired in repose. We are made holy that we may witness—in fact, that is the very first reason given for the gift of the Spirit (Acts i, 7, 8). The boldness of Peter and John was the most noticeable result of Pentecost, and God's greatest immediate need is for men and women who will propagate the good news.

This also we cannot do with enticing words of human wisdom, but only as the Spirit demonstrates His power (1 Cor. ii, 4).

Are we then to sit back and let God do His work with no effort on our part? By no means. God does not overthrow the mechanism of human personality which He created; He works through our will and our devotion, and our intensest efforts will be required. "Strive," says Christ; "run, contend, fight, endure, mortify, press on," echoes His great apostle. "Ye have not yet resisted unto blood, striving against sin," is the reproach of the writer to the Hebrews (xii, 4). But our striving is a striving of faith, just as our conversion was a conversion of faith (Col. ii, 6), and faith is the gift of God. Our most agonized strivings, our most resolute renunciations, our most fervent devotions are God-given; God often needs to bring us to our extremity before He has His opportunity. Just because our sanctification is of faith, so it is of no merit before God. We do not deserve anything from God, and without God we can do nothing. We are not earning God's favour—we are merely doing what is our duty to do. For the same reason we are not duty-driven; we are giving God the service of our lives out of the love of our hearts which He has first poured into us. God is not defying the laws of our nature, making us work otherwise than in the way we were made. We do things because we want to do them, out of love, perhaps, for someone else; we enjoy a difficult task and find pleasure in achieving it; we like to exercise our minds on a problem and to master it. This is how God works; first He makes us to love our Saviour, as we gaze upon His Cross, and to recognize our sinfulness; then we see the Cross as a place where we too must die, where God has made an end of sin. By faith we hold ourselves in that position, crucified with Christ and dead to sin (Gal. ii, 20). Then out of love to Christ we set about putting this into practice; by His help we establish good habits; out of joy we learn to worship and there grows in us a desire to know more of Him and His ways; our minds are extended in the study of the Bible and the application of its principles to our problems; and through it all we dare to believe that God has us in hand and is working out His purpose in us. We grow appreciative of the needs of others; we experience something of the Saviour's love for the lost; and so we are constrained to pass on the message of liberation. In short, we work *out* our own salvation with fear and trembling, for it is God who works *in* us, both to *will* and to *do* of His good pleasure (Phil. ii, 12, 13).

This is the ideal, and there is no reason why we should not attain it. There are two things that will hinder us in reaching it: an unwillingness to admit the Life-giving Spirit into every department of our lives—in fact, to acknowledge Him truly as Lord; and the more subtle pride which continually uproots the plant to see how it is growing and boasts of its achievements which are not its own at all. But God will have all of us, and He knows how to abase the proud, though we shall suffer in the process.

Perhaps this all seems very intricate and difficult; perhaps it would have been better not to have tried to explain the intimate relationship between the Christian and the Spirit of God. To anyone who feels like that, I would say this. The Holy Spirit's work is to point to Jesus. We are not made to devote ourselves to anyone or anything which is pure Spirit. It is not natural, which is one reason why the subject of this chapter is difficult to make simple. We are flesh and blood, and by our bodies we express ourselves. God knows this, and so He came as Jesus in a human body. We can love Jesus, and strive to be like Him. We can understand His sacrifice and His horror of sin. We can think of Him in Heaven with all power to help us. We can ask Him into our hearts and treat Him as our companion. We know He has lived our life and understands our troubles. So we can look to Him in time of need, and pray to Him and sing His praises. And that is sanctification; for as we do that, as St. Paul tells us, we are changed by the Spirit into His image (2 Cor. iii, 18).

We have thought of the work of the Spirit in an isolated Christian, but no Christian is isolated, and he gains much from the experience and fellowship of others. It is not good for man to be alone, and every Christian is made by the Spirit into a part of a great fellowship, the Church of Christ. It is

70

the special work of the Spirit to create this organism, born a living thing on the day of Pentecost, and to add individual believers to it. Through it He speaks to the outside world; it is said to be His earthly temple, built of stones to which He has given life (Eph. ii, 21, 22). This is the subject of our next chapter, but there is another matter we must touch on first—the work of the Spirit in giving us God's written revelation in the Bible.

The Bible is a remarkable book. Compiled from writings separated in time by at least 1,500 years, it displays a remarkable unity. Superficial discrepancies give place on careful study to an ever-deepening wonder at its unity of outlook, its unique view of God and man, its thorough going honesty in its portrayal of human character, refusing to flatter even the nation and persons of its own writers. Further, it displays a remarkable consistency in its terminology, so that often the best guide to the meaning of a word is its usage by other Biblical writers; and a singular freedom from commonly accepted, but erroneous, speculations of the time in which it was written. Truly this is God's book. It reveals to us the mind and working of God in a way in which no other book does. Here may the voice of God be found. Yet at the same time it is man's book. It is written in human languages by men with diverse styles and characters; it describes the actions of good men and bad, and voices the thoughts of Job's misguided comforters and the disillusioned Preacher alongside of the praises of David and the messages of the prophets with their "thus saith the Lord". It is God's revelation mediated through the forms of human thought. Also it reveals God by stages as man is able to receive Him, so that while there is no erroneous revelation in the earlier books which has to be corrected later, yet man at first does many things with God's seeming approval which later standards would condemn simply because God expects people to live up to the light that they have.

We are thus faced with the same problem we have met with twice already—the inter-relation of the human and the divine. Whether it be in the Person of Christ, in the sanctification of the believer, or in the writing of the Bible, it is impossible to dissect out God's work from man's. It is God *through* man, and man *by* God, not God *and* man side by side. Jesus was a human baby, but every element of His personality was divine. The Christian must follow after holiness with all his heart, but the whole is the work of God's Spirit. So in the Bible man writes with all diligence and to the best of his ability, but the whole is the living word of God. This is the phenomenon of inspiration. There are two instructive passages about it in the New Testament; St. Paul tells us that all scripture is "breathed of God" (2 Tim. iii, 16), and St. Peter that "Holy men of God spake as they were driven by the Holy Spirit" (2 Pet. i, 21). The ship was a human writer, steered by the rudder of his will, but the wind that filled his sails was the very Breath of God, the Holy Spirit. So he was borne along, in a manner almost independent of his own efforts, as Paul's ship scudded before the gale from Crete to Malta (the word is the same in the Greek). God impelled men to write what He had just revealed to them, held them on the course, preserved them from error, and through them gave His message to the world. As Amos says: "The Lord God hath spoken, who can but prophesy?" (Amos iii, 8).

There are two errors to be avoided in thinking of inspiration. On the one hand the writers were not mere shorthand-typists, writing down what God had dictated. The lecture method of instruction has sometimes been cynically described as a way of transferring material from the note-book of the lecturer to that of the student without its passing through the mind of either. God never works like that; He uses and energizes the living active minds of His servants. On the other hand we must not go to the other extreme and think that they are just giving us their ideas about God. They are telling us what God has told them, through history, through worship, through personal experience, and when they say "thus saith the Lord" they are not using idle words. The Holy Spirit worked in and through the writers of the Bible in a way in which He has not worked before or since.

This means the revelation is authoritative and final. It

derives its authority from God through its writers, who were recognized as His spokesmen. Christ Himself ratified for us the authority of the Old Testament, and by anticipation commissioned His disciples to add to it in the New. The Church did not give the books their authoritative position; she recognized it as already inherent in them by virtue of the authority of Christ and His apostles. So the Bible becomes for us the standard with which we can test what men say about God. If only Christians would apply the simple test for which Isaiah appealed, there would be a sharp reduction in the number of strange and ephemeral sects! "To the law and to the testimony!" is his cry; "if they speak not according to this word, surely there is no morning for them" (Isa. viii, 20, R.V.).

When we say the Bible is the Word of God we must be clear what we mean. We mean that it bears God's imprimatur of authority. To reject its writers is to reject Him, for He inspired their work. We do not mean that every phrase in it is God's message in every conceivable circumstance. Shutting one's eyes, opening a page at random, and lighting on a text with a pin is not a reasonable method of arriving at God's will—in fact, it is nothing more or less than pagan superstition. The Bible contains the record of the words and deeds of many types of men. We are to read it with intelligence. Above all we need the Holy Spirit to make it plain to us. He inspired its writers, and He has never left the book since. He has preserved it for us, watched over its countless transcriptions and translations, and now when we open it He is at hand to explain His own work. It will repay the most careful study. As we read, God will speak to us, for every part of it is a true record of God's dealings with man. It has been tried in limitless ways and has never been found wanting. No wonder the Devil has attacked it, for it is the Christian's daily food. By it he learns of his Master and of himself; all the wonderful message of redemption is found in it, and by it his Christian life is maintained.[1]

[1] For a note on Bible Difficulties, see Appendix IV.

CHAPTER VIII

THE GROWING CHURCH

THE Bible begins in a garden with a man and his wife hiding from God. It ends in a city with many gates, but one street. God's programme culminates in a community with a common life and interest—as has been well said, we must all walk in the same street in heaven. The individual must personally enlist in the army of the King, but he then becomes a member of a body of men whose function is to serve their Captain to the utmost of their power.

The word 'body' is suggestive and significant, for in the New Testament the Church is called the Body of Christ. That tells us several things about the Church: first, it is a living unity, not a man-made organization. In fact, it is an *organism*. Now in all many-celled organisms, including the human body, each cell is differentiated from the others according to the duty it is required to perform, while each carries a nucleus which marks it as belonging to that body and no other, and which organizes its activities to the good of the whole. So it is in the Body of Christ; every individual Christian is entitled to the name and to his place in the Body because he has in him the Holy Spirit of God; so that he is related to all other Christians as brothers in Christ, fellow-members of the Body, yet has his own specific part to play in the building up of the Body and in carrying out its work. He is not a member of Christ because he has "joined the body"; the human body deals ruthlessly enough with any foreign material which tries to intrude itself; rather he is added to the Body because he belongs to Christ.

Secondly, the Body grows as new cells are continually added to it. In the physical world they are derived from individual cells of the body by division, but in the spiritual Body they are added by the Spirit by the miracle of new birth which links them with the Head. Thirdly, the Body is dominated by one single mind and moves with a single purpose. It is the instrument of its Head, by which He expresses Himself. Christ is in the world now in the person of His Church, and through her He is working out His triumphal programme.

The Church we have been considering—the Body of Christ—is the true Church which the New Testament describes, consisting of all those who have put their trust in Christ and have been made His by the Spirit who has come to live in their hearts. In its perfect state it includes all Christians, past, present and future. In a sense it began when first John and Andrew left the Baptist to follow Christ (John i, 37), but those were days of transition, and it could not take on its full character until the day of Pentecost when the Holy Spirit came to make the individual disciples into the Church of God. It incorporates also the faithful warriors of Old Testament days who trusted God and looked forward to the completion of His purpose (Heb. xii, 23).

The word Church, however, is used in many other senses, some necessary for the understanding of God's purposes, others wholly misleading. We speak of the Early Church, the Church at Corinth, the Methodist Church, St. Matthew's Church; and the man in the street is apt to say "Our John is going in for the Church," or "the Church ought to make its services more popular," when he means something very different from the Church of Christ.

The New Testament gives us a precedent for speaking about local churches, like the Church in Jerusalem, or the Church in the house of Gaius, or about the Church on earth at any one time. But we must remember that the Church is made up of men and women, not of bricks and mortar, and though we may set apart a building for God's service and call it a Church, that is not what the New Testament means by a Church. Rather what is all-important is the people who meet in it. It is strange how many people will be most particular that their women-folk should wear hats or tie a scarf over their heads when entering a church building when no service is in progress, who nevertheless never think of acknowledging God in family prayers or even of saying grace before meals. One is reminded of our Lord's attitude to the Pharisees, who tithed mint and aniseed (Matt. xxiii, 23). Instinctively we feel that a church building is 'sacred', but we should be hard put to it to find any scriptural warrant for our behaviour. It is the people who meet there who make the Church, not its beauty or its associations. God is with five humble Christians praying round their fireside in a far more intimate way than He is in the grandest cathedral thronged with sightseers. It is possible to be unduly distressed about war-damaged churches; it is a tragedy when houses set apart for the worship of God are destroyed, but it is far more serious if His worshippers have their souls undermined by moral excess and blasted by hatred or the snare of sudden wealth. Let us retain our sense of perspective.

Still less is the Church of God to be equated with the clergy. They are the servants of the Church, not its overlords. It is not fair to sit back and expect the bishops to back up this or that plan for social reform; or to criticize the local parson or minister for not getting on with his job; every Christian is called upon to play his part in the work of the Church of which he is a member. Nor can he pass on his responsibility for personal Christian growth to his pastors; God means each of us to have personal dealings with Himself. There is much confusion nowadays as to the true position of ministers in the Church. The New Testament makes it plain that they are men to whom God has given special gifts of preaching and teaching, and of "feeding the flock of God." The Bible is their authority, and every Christian may test their utterances by it. They are not 'go-betweens' between a man and God, for there is only one Mediator, the one God has provided, Jesus Christ. To Him personally we are all directly united.

If, then, God's true Church is composed of all true Christians and no others, how is it that looking about us we see something so very different? Hundreds of divided sects, some scarcely Christian, some claiming that they only are the Church of Christ: numbers of people who would be deeply offended at the suggestion that they were not Christians, but who nevertheless know nothing of the experience of the new birth: and a countless number, especially in a country such as ours, whose only acquaintance with a Church is that they are carried in twice, to be christened and buried, and walk in once to the pagan strains of Wagner.

Fully to answer this would require a lengthy excursion into Church history, but we can see without looking very deeply that the visible Church of professing Christians can never be co-extensive with the true Church, the blessed company of all faithful people. Wheat and tares grow together in God's field, and He alone can accurately distinguish them—in fact, we are forbidden to adopt any rigid policy of exclusion, because the criteria of the true Christian are largely invisible and human judgment is so often mistaken. While hypocrisy remains a besetting sin of the religious man, and while humble men and women find mercy with the Saviour when they are yet ignorant or misguided on matters which Churches, often quite rightly, require of their members, so long will the outward Church differ from the Body of Christ both by inclusion and omission. From the days of Ananias and Apollos it has been so.

Against this we must set down the notable achievements of the Church which are going on before our very eyes. The gospel of Jesus Christ is at long last being taken to every nation under heaven; in face of persecution there has arisen a remarkable unity of spirit among the Churches of Europe; great interdenominational missions and movements, such as that in South India, draw together true Christians from many different sects. The unity of the Body is a fact which every member feels to be real and vital; he knows the divisions are only superficial, though to the world without they appear deep and wide.

This distinction between the true and the visible Church does not imply that we believe in two separate Churches. There is one Church, regarded from two different points of view. Man sees the visible Church, the companies of professing Christians. God sees the true Church, the one living Body of Christ. We are not called upon to distinguish them rather, as St. Paul did in his letters, are we to address people as they profess themselves to be, at the same time warning of the great dangers of a hollow profession and the sinfulness of hypocrisy. This may also help us to understand the words we say in the Creed: "I believe in one catholic and apostolic Church." The existence of such a Church is a matter of faith, for the Church to which these four "marks" apply cannot be identified with any visible community: it is the true Church of God. But these four characteristics are ideals towards which the visible Church must strive, and of which some degree of attainment must accompany any claim to be a Christian Church at all. Christians are called to show fellowship and unity with all who profess the name of Christ: they are called to live holy lives, and as a Church have a right to exclude notorious unrepentant sinners from fellowship: they are to preach the gospel to all nations—for this is true catholicity —and to girdle the world with their prayers: they are to be loyal to the teaching of the apostles, and as a Church to be guided by the New Testament and administer the Sacraments as therein laid down.

As we trace the course of the visible Church down the ages we cannot do better than look briefly at Christ's own inspired pictures of her history recorded for us in the seven parables of Matthew xiii. Here are seven pictures of the Church which are true for all time; yet many Christians have felt that they give in order of time the aspects of the Church's character which have been successively brought to the fore in the actual course of her history. First comes the wide sowing of the Word with its diverse results, as seen in the book of Acts and the missionary activity of the sub-apostolic age. The cares of this world and the active persecution of Satanic powers were the great enemies of the Church's growth. Then came a great change, when Constantine made Christianity the state religion of the Roman Empire. Multitudes of mere political adherents were swept through the waters of baptism: a sowing of tares took place on a scale without precedent, though, alas, not without sequel. The Church grew and spread in the most luxuriant manner, but this was not without its dangers. Within the branches of this vast growth there lurked those very pagan elements that had previously tried to snatch away the precious seed. It is a tragic fact that at this time many pagan customs became part and parcel of Christian practice. (To mention only one—why is it that we celebrate our Lord's birthday at the winter solstice with holly and mistletoe, Yule logs, revelry and exchanging of gifts?) Then followed a more subtle attack from the foe: the official teaching of the Church, which had hitherto remained largely true to her New Testament charter, began to undergo a change, until in the Middle Ages forgiveness could be bought and sold, God's message of life was withheld from those who wished to read it, and man presumed to command his Master to descend upon his altar and there be reoffered for the sins of His people: indeed, even for those who were thought to have died in faith but to have not yet attained to the blessedness of His Presence. The leaven of false teaching had permeated the lump.

But there is another side to this gloomy picture, which soon would once again emerge to view. One here, one there, found entrance by faith alone into the kingdom of Heaven, and, often at the cost of their lives, began to make known again the gate to eternal life for which the Master laid down His life on the Cross. New life surged through the world of Christendom; once more God's precious Word was read and studied, and its truth drove men to reform their Church at home, and then to travel far and wide over the earth to call men and women to the only Saviour. The sleeping Church awoke to a great unfinished task, a task that is unfinished still. Yet through the centuries, and especially within the last two hundred years, the net has been cast in ever-widening circles, and from east and west, north and south, they come from all nations to take their places in the kingdom of God.

This is the primary mission of the Church of Christ, and this is her Lord's last command to her. "Go," He bids us, as St. Matthew records it, "and make disciples of all nations, baptizing them . . . and teaching them. . . ." (Matt. xxviii, 19, 20). Repentance and remission of sins in His Name is the burden of our message (Luke xxiv, 47). In short, the

Body of Christ is called to grow by self-extension, by evangelization throughout the world. We are Christ's instrument by which He expresses Himself and does His work in the world today, and that work is first and foremost the perfecting and completion of His Body.

We are here to preach to all the world, but we are not here to convert the world. There will always be some who fail to respond. Wheat and tares, good fish and bad, continue till the end of time. We are not called to be hermits or isolationists, but collaborators with God in the great work of redemption. This means that first of all we must find fellowship in some way with other Christians. God needs team work. A man told a famous preacher once that he could not find any church which suited him: he didn't agree with the teaching of this one, that one was too sleepy, here the parson did so many questionable things, there he was too narrow-minded, and so on. "Are you looking for a perfect Church, then?" said the preacher. "Yes." "Well, if you find it, don't join it, or you will spoil it!" As Bishop Blunt says, if the Church still has spots and wrinkles on its face (Eph. v, 27) we must take our share of responsibility for putting them there. The Church needs *us* . . . if we are alive unto God.

Secondly, the presence of the Church in the world, however imperfect the Church, and however pagan the world, should have *some* effect on everyone. Unquestionably it has had. The world owes its moral standard, its social services, its philanthropy, its views of God, however imperfect, to the influence of Christians in its midst. It is impossible to conceive how impoverished the world would be if the Christians were all removed from it at the moment of their conversion. This effect we may call, if we like, the secondary mission of the Church.

Our Lord gives, in the Sermon on the Mount, three luminous illustrations of the place of His Church in the world. Strictly speaking, there was as yet no Church when these words were uttered, but they are addressed to all in whose lives the reign of God is demonstrated, and that for us is in the Christian Church. We are, He says, the salt of the earth, the light of the world, a city set on a hill (Matt. v, 13, 14). Salt, the light of a candle, a hillside village: all familiar things to His listeners, yet profoundly significant for us. First, the Church is like *salt*. Salt is valued in the East for flavour, and as a preservative. We may see in this the Church's unmistakable moral tang; the standards she upholds are meant to exercise a restraining and purifying influence on all she touches.

Then we are to shine as *lights*, so that men may see our good works. The Christian is not to be neglectful of good works; the light he is to shine into the darkness about him is not only the light of the gospel, it is also the light of his own good deeds. We must not think we have done our duty if we merely preach to the poor and the oppressed; they will have little to say to the glory of our Father unless we apply ourselves unpatronizingly and sympathetically to their problems and perplexities.

Finally we are limned as a *city* set on a hill—perhaps like some village perched on a hillside which our Lord's vast audience could see; its daily life lived in the public eye under the open heaven: the women at their doors in the morning grinding their corn, the busy market thronged with traffic, the judges sitting in the gate, girls with their water-pots returning from the well. We are, in fact, to be a public example of God's ideal community. This is our contribution to civics. We are not the state—though it also is God's minister, and as individuals we may share in its work. But as a Church we are an example to the state, demonstrating the abiding principles of citizenship, and showing how it is possible for brethren to live together in unity when actuated by the love of Christ and the power of His Spirit. How far we fall short of these three God-given pictures!

But we are not left without help from our Leader. He has His regular lines of communication by which supplies may be brought to us. True, at any time we may establish direct communication with Him through His Spirit who lives within us; but we are creatures of habit with material bodies, and it is essential that we should use His regular ways of obtaining advice and supplies. The Church calls them her 'means of grace', but she does not provide them. God has given them to her, and she is their recipient; she has to keep her end open, as it were. There are many of them, but we will consider six of the more important.

(1) *Prayer.*

Prayer is as important to the Christian as the air he breathes; in fact, this 'line of communication' is almost a bottle-neck, for all the others depend upon it to a greater or less extent. In prayer the Christian is in his Master's immediate presence; he speaks to God and God to him. The condition of the availability of this channel of communication is faith—"he that cometh to God must *believe* that He is, and that He is a rewarder of them that diligently seek Him" (Heb. xi, 6). Prayer has its public and its private aspects: we may pray at any time, but we should set apart a time for regular private prayer; and we should join together with others in public prayer for which a special blessing is promised (Matt. xviii, 19, 20). Only through the Spirit can we truly pray (Rom. viii, 26).

The practice of prayer raises a number of problems in the minds of some Christians. There is not space here to enter fully into these, but a few remarks must suffice. First, no-one who has followed thus far will suppose that prayer is a way of getting our will done in Heaven—it is a way of getting God's will done on earth. So that, although God promises always to hear and answer the prayer of faith, the answer is often "Wait," and may be "No". He knows what is best for us. Secondly, the effect of prayer is not merely subjective. It is, indeed, a way of attuning my will to the divine harmony, but it is more than that. When a Christian prays in faith, something happens which would not have happened had he not prayed. This is what makes prayer such a valuable weapon in our armoury. How, then, can we say that God does not change His mind nor man deflect His purpose? Because in the purpose of God the means as well as the ends are included: God determines to do certain things in answer to our prayers. The supposition, "if we had not prayed," is in a way meaningless; God takes our prayers into His reckoning. We believe that, in God's plan, what is to be will be, not that what is to be won't be! In the words that Julian of Norwich tells us she heard her Lord speaking to her: "I am the ground of thy beseeching; first it is My will that thou have it; and after, I make thee to will it; and after, I make thee beseech it; and thou beseechest it. How should it then be that thou shouldst not have thy beseeching?"[1]

(2) *Bible Reading*.

The Bible reveals to us God's plan of campaign, and through it we may receive our marching orders. All we know about God comes to us through its pages, so that it is the supreme authority for all our thinking about Him. But it is no dead letter; it can be to us the living word of God, speaking to our immediate needs. Again, we need our own regular times of private reading, and also as a Church we read the Scripture in public as our authority, for instruction, and as a testimony to its place in our religion. Again, the condition of its usefulness to us is our faith and obedience and our prayer for the Spirit's illumination.

(3) *Worship*.

God seeks for worshippers (John iv, 23), because by means of worship our vision is enlarged and we grow like the object of our worship. We cannot help worshipping: it is instinctive in us; but God asks that this instinct which He implanted be directed to Himself. Only through the Spirit—God active in us—can we truly worship Him.

In worship we occupy ourselves with the greatness of God. We can worship as we enjoy the wonder of God's creation; we can worship as we read in the Bible of the depth of God's love and the purity of His holiness; but most of all we are called upon to meet together as Christians for the worship of God (Heb. x, 25). Here essentially we find our fellowship as a Church as we unite in praise of our common Saviour. Great music, great beauty, great art of all kinds may draw out our worship of its Creator, but most of all when it is directed to a common service of praise. Increased likeness to God is the grace of worship; we grow like what we look at (2 Cor. iii, 18).

[1] Quoted by Amy Carmichael, *Gold Cord*, p. 49 (S.P.C.K.).

(4) *Preaching*.

This is an important means which God uses to build up His Church. He has appointed it as the way by which His message is to be spread and His will for Christians made known. There are the same conditions and safeguards: His Word in the Bible is the standard of truth (Isa. viii, 20; Acts xvii, 11), His Spirit in the preacher the essential motive power (1 Cor. ii, 4, 5), and faith in the hearer the condition of the availability of God's message to his understanding (Rom. x, 14-17; Heb. iv, 2). So much 'preaching' today is mere moral exhortation; but our great need is exposition of the Word of God.

There are two further ways in which God's grace may be appropriated by His people, which commonly go by the name of Sacraments. The word Sacrament means a pledge or oath, and could loosely be applied to any token of God's favour to us or any act on our part of allegiance to Christ. Strictly, however, the term is confined to those acts which Christ has personally commanded us to perpetuate, in which a material sign or token is used to assist our faith in the appropriation of God's grace. There are thus two Sacraments: Baptism and the Lord's Supper. They are essentially public acts in which the whole Church is called to participate. As in the other four "means of grace" considered, without the vitalizing power of the Spirit producing faith in the recipient, they are empty and valueless formalities. God's grace is always available for us on the same conditions; it is simply His continued unchanging character toward us, not a kind of spiritual petrol laid on only at certain points on the road. The Sacraments help us to realize the conditions; they are not pipes which charge us up with power, but rather warrants or title-deeds which assure us of our right to claim God's benefits when we will. Let us consider them in turn.

(5) *Baptism*.

The sign here is water, which pictures to us God's offer of cleansing from sin by burial of our old life in the waters and rising again to a new life with Christ (Rom. vi, 1-6); in other words, what we have called regeneration. The work of God's Spirit in regeneration is in practice seldom contemporaneous with the sign. There are two different views of Baptism among Christians. One group of Christians give the sign of Baptism only to adults *after* evidence of real regeneration of heart has been shown, thereby strengthening their faith with this tangible pledge of God's cleansing and forgiveness. Others give the sign also to children of Christian parents *before* there can be any evidence of regeneration, while they arc yet infants, emphasizing God's covenant with the family as a unit, and with the sign strengthening the parents' faith that if they fulfil their share of the covenant God will accept and in His own time regenerate their child. There is no conclusive evidence as to New Testament practice, and we do well to allow latitude of interpretation in this matter between fellow-Christians.

(6) *The Lord's Supper.*

This Sacrament should be exceedingly precious to us all. Here, as nowhere else, do we realize our fellowship and unity as members of Christ's Church. Unhappily, it has been hedged about with the thorns of controversy, and bitter divisions have arisen on its account. In spite of our Lord's warning against a literal interpretation of His words (John vi, 63), the Sacrament has been made mechanical, and the essential work of the Holy Spirit in the heart of the recipient has been forgotten.

Nowhere is it more important to remember that this is God's gift to us, not ours to Him. We are not offering Him a gift, still less a sacrifice; we come as guests to God's board. It is the Sacrament of the Lord's Supper: our risen Master gives us bread and wine that we may remember His Cross and Passion; we look *back* to the night when He first gave His disciples the tokens of His love, and transformed the Passover, memorial of their deliverance from Egypt, into the memorial of our deliverance from sin. Then it is a Holy Communion: a common participation in the grace of God. We look *up* together as a Church to our ascended Head, and by faith

85

make Him our very life, realizing the presence of His Spirit in our hearts. Finally, it is our Eucharist: our act of thanksgiving when we worship the Father and offer Him our praises for His salvation and our lives for His service; we look *on* to the day of final triumph and pledge our loyalty to His victorious purpose. It is our sacrament, our soldiers' oath; we show the Lord's death till He come (1 Cor. xi, 26).

The Sacraments may be thought of as being like a wedding-ring; they are Christ's gifts to His bride, which He expects her to accept and wear. They pledge His love to us, and ours to Him. They are not the essence of our relationship to Him; that is an inner intimate matter entered on by an act of solemn troth. But they are normally expected of us as part of our Christian witness. Christ expects us to accept these tokens of His love to us, and the world expects us to declare in this way that we are His. Right use of them will reduce the danger of flirting with the world's attractions, but only if they represent to Him and us our inner devotion to our Lord and Saviour Jesus Christ.

These are some of the ways in which God helps those who would share in His plans. Some are very simple, material and even commonplace: a book, a humble preacher, water, bread and wine. But these are things amid which our lives are lived, our battles fought; and God comes down to meet us where we are. The leap of faith is made as narrow as can be— "The Word is very nigh thee, in thy mouth, and in thy heart" (Deut. xxx, 14). And the climax of it all is that our great Commander, now sitting in Heaven as our representative, will one day Himself step down and visit the battlefield to lead His people into the victory He has won.

CHAPTER IX

THE RETURNING KING

THROUGHOUT the Bible, both in the Old and New Testaments, we are continually being impressed with the fact that God has a plan for the world whose climax is in the future, and that human history is moving forward to this goal. It is writ large, of course, in the pages of the Old Testament prophets that their visions related to what was in their future, since the tremendous events associated with the Incarnation of Jesus Christ were yet ahead of them. But when we turn to the New Testament we find that although the writers declare that many of these visions are now fulfilled, they throw others forward yet again into the future. Since the whole question of the fulfilment of Old Testament prophecy is an important one, it is worthy of a brief discussion.

We must first understand that the primary message of the Old Testament prophets was addressed to the people of their own day, and arose out of their immediate circumstances and needs. It is a mistake, therefore, to intrude an allegorical or predictive element into their words unnecessarily. Nevertheless these prophetic "sermons" are shot through and through with reminders of Israel's glorious future which cannot be dismissed as vague aspirations. It is best to illustrate from a particular passage, and Isaiah ii-iv will serve our purpose well enough.

The passage begins (ii, 1-4) with a description of the "latter days" when all nations will come to Mount Zion to learn God's law, and, as a consequence, war will be abolished. This is probably a quotation from the contemporary prophet Micah which Isaiah has taken as his "text". In immediate contrast there follows a description of the present state of the people of Judah with their corruption and idolatry. The prophet points out that the judgment of God must fall on them for this, before the ideal can be attained. He concludes (iv, 2-6) with a new depiction of the future which penetrates more deeply into the way in which the opening vision can be attained. It speaks of a holy remnant in Zion, forgiven and purged by the Spirit of judgment.

Broadly this is the message of all the prophets. There is a day coming which will be a day of judgment for the heathen and for the unfaithful in Israel, but a day of great blessing for the faithful remnant of God's people, and through them to the rest of the world. Israel is to be punished with exile and scattering as a penalty for her sins, but God will gather her again and make her a blessing.

Parallel with these there are the prophecies of the coming Messiah and His kingdom, beginning with Isaiah ix, and of the Suffering Servant, which we discussed in Chapter V. The question immediately arises in the mind of anyone who accepts the divine inspiration of the prophets (which they repeatedly claim): how much of this has been fulfilled? The New Testament and Christian experience can help us to find an answer.

It is plain first of all that the coming of Christ and the growth of the Christian Church has fulfilled a good deal. In Luke xxiv, 27, our Lord began from Moses and all the prophets and interpreted the things concerning Himself. In Acts iii, 24, Peter can say that "all the prophets, as many as have spoken, have foretold of these days". In Romans xvi, 26, the Apostle Paul declares that the mystery of the gospel is made known unto all nations through the scriptures of the prophets. So then we shall not be far wrong if we look in the prophets for predictions of the coming of Christ and the triumphs of the gospel. It is clear that He is both the Suffering Servant and the Messianic King. To look no further than the chapter we have already referred to, it is evident that Peter implies as much in Acts iii, 13-14, by the titles Servant and Prince which he gives to Jesus. But James, the Lord's brother, goes further, and in Acts xv, 14-18, applies the words of Amos (ix, 11-12) about the restoration of David's fallen tent, and the consequent seeking after God by the Gentiles, to the opening of the door of gospel opportunity to the Gentiles in the days in which he was speaking. The passage from Amos is altogether similar to that we have discussed in Isaiah ii. Yet quite plainly the days of universal peace there depicted have not come. Can the New Testament give us any light about this?

The answer it gives is that the coming of Christ has brought in a new age. In this age will be fulfilled all that the old age looked forward to. This is the "age to come" whose powers (Heb. vi, 5) have been seen on earth since the days of Calvary and Pentecost. The Cross is, as we might say, the "king-pin" which links this age to the age to come (ci. Heb. ix, 26). But this new age has a consummation which is associated with the return of the King, when the complete fulfilment will be seen. When the Lord Jesus was caught up into the clouds on the Mount of Olives the two angelic attendants promised His return in language which could not possibly refer to the out-pouring of the Holy Spirit. "This same Jesus, which is taken up from you into heaven, shall so come in like manner as ye have seen Him go into heaven" (Acts i, 11). This is the only view which makes sense of the present turmoil of world affairs. The battle with evil is plainly not yet won. Deliverance has been widespread, though it is not yet universal, nor in any one human soul is it complete. God must and will intervene a second time. How then will this intervention take place?

"In like manner as ye have seen Him go," said the angels on the day of His ascension. That is to say, visibly, bodily, gloriously. He came as a helpless babe: He went as a conqueror to sit at the Father's right hand. As a conqueror, as He Himself tells us, He will return (Matt. xxiv, 30). We cannot tell when He will come. The world will be going on as usual, and many will be taken unawares, but come He will. We know only what He has told us, and He wants us to be ready at all times, so He has not told us precisely when it will be. We have a task to complete, the task of proclaiming His good news of salvation to the world. When all have heard and His Body is complete, He will come.

It is natural to ask how His coming will fulfil the prophecies of the Bible and bring in the golden age. But any answer to this question raises difficulties. It is not that the New Testament gives no answer: in fact it makes a number of very plain statements. But the links which are necessary before we can construct any definite scheme of events are given disconnectedly, or through symbolism, in such a way that only the events themselves will interpret them for us. It was so at Christ's first coming: the Old Testament had said sufficient to enable people to recognize the Messiah after He came, but not enough to construct a chart of events beforehand. This must, I think, be taken as deliberate. It is not for us to know times and seasons, and we are wise not to attempt it (Acts i, 7). The New Testament writers lay stress on the spiritual applications of our Lord's return.

Even with regard to the broad outline of God's purpose Christians have held very different opinions. One view which has been widely held all down the centuries appeals to the parable of the wicked husbandmen, and to such verses as Gal. iii, 29, and Heb. xiii, 22, as showing that the promises to Israel are now being implemented in their only real sense, that is, in the spiritual blessings of the Christian Church. The Jews have been scattered since the fall of Jerusalem, but they will be gathered one by one as they are converted and made members of the Church of God. The Apostle Paul in Romans xi, 12, 25, 26, implies that they will be converted in large numbers as the age closes, and that this will be a great triumph of the gospel and blessing to the world. In this case the "millennium" of popular parlance—the thousand years of Rev. xx—may be a symbol of this time of blessing. Christ's reign grows and extends until all are subject to Him, and death, the last enemy, is destroyed by being swallowed up in resurrection at His return (1 Cor. xv, 25-26; 1 Thess. iv, 16).

Others, especially in recent years, expect a literal restoration of the Jews to Palestine, over whom the returning Christ will reign in person. The first resurrection (of Christians only) and the thousand years of Rev. xx are then literal events. There is a hint of two separate resurrections in John v, 29, and the apostle Paul describes the resurrection of Christians as "from among the dead" (Phil. iii, 11). The wicked dead do not then rise until after the millennial reign.

There is probably truth in both views, and certainly both meet with difficulties. We must not lose sight of the plain facts which our Lord has told us. His coming will be unexpected, at least by the majority. There will be some, perhaps many on earth, who will dread Him, because they are living in opposition to His will (Matt. xxiv, 36-51). He will rally the Church to His standard, and first in their ranks will be those who have died in faith in Christ. This we are expressly told (1 Thess. iv, 15-17). His living servants will follow to complete His body the Church; from all the earth they will come, caught up from the four winds of heaven (Matt. xxiv, 31, 40, 41). The enemies of Christ are finally overwhelmed, and Christ reigns triumphant. Whether there be one or two resurrections, all men will ultimately be raised to stand before God (Matt. xxv, 32; Rev. xx, 12).

It is important that we understand clearly what Christians mean by the resurrection of the dead. We do not mean mere survival of the soul. That is a pagan notion, and the Bible has practically nothing to say about the souls of men apart from their bodies.[1] Nor do we mean the reconstitution of this physical body. We receive a new body, like the risen body of Christ (Phil. iii, 21). St. Paul calls it a "spiritual" body (1 Cor. xv, 44) and a "building of God not made with hands" (2 Cor. v, 1), which is a way of saying it is quite different from anything we have experienced. Yet there is identity, and recognition, and we shall have a more, not a less, perfect medium for the expression of our personality. In it we shall be judged for the deeds done in this body.

Judgment is the culmination of God's dealings with this world. Whether we like it or not, it must be so. God's programme moves to a crisis, a division, a judgment. If it does not, there are two alternatives. Either evil is triumphant, Calvary was a farce, the Christian is deluded, and God is defeated—which is so unthinkable that no-one has ever

---

[1] It is idle to speculate what happens to the souls of men between death and resurrection; presumably they pass out of temporal relationships altogether, so that the question is probably meaningless. The Christian is assured that death brings to him the immediate presence of Christ (Luke xxiii, 43; Phil. i, 23).

proposed it; or else Satan is repentant, and all men, past and present, will have as many chances as they like until ultimately love and obedience to God is born in their hearts. I suppose we would all like to believe this; to quote one recent writer: "I would pay any price to be able to say truthfully, 'All will be saved'. But my reason retorts, 'Without their will, or with it?' If I say 'Without their will' I at once perceive a contradiction; how can the supreme voluntary act of self-surrender be involuntary? If I say 'With their will', my reason replies, 'How if they *will not* give in?' " (C. S. Lewis, *Problem of Pain*, p. 107. The whole chapter on Hell is most penetrating and challenging). In a word, if God has decreed to limit Himself, as He has, by allowing a creature with free will to fall into rebellion, that free will does not make sense unless at any rate some creatures are allowed to pursue the road of rebellion to the end. None, indeed, can ever turn to God except by His grace shown toward them, but Calvary is incomprehensible, unless the fate from which it has saved us is an accessible one. In any event, Christ Himself most clearly told us that final rebellion was the awful state of many of mankind, and that in this life only have we opportunity to accept His grace in salvation (Matt. xxv, 41; Luke xvi, 19-31).

This judgment is on the borders of eternity, and its consequences are eternal. St. Peter tells us that this universe itself, the abode of sin and rebellion, will be dissolved in fire and replaced (2 Pet. iii, 10-13). Here again we are confronted by symbolism, but it must mean the complete severance of the eternal order from that which we now know. In that eternal order there is a state called heaven, and there is a state which our Lord calls hell. Hell, or Gehenna, was the valley outside Jerusalem where the rubbish was consigned to an undying bonfire. Our Lord also describes it as 'outer darkness'—outside the eternal realm which is filled with the light of God. St. Paul describes it as "eternal destruction from the presence of the Lord" (2 Thess. i, 9). We know, then, that it is irrevocable, and God is not there. Satan and his fellow-rebels will be there, and men who are involved in his rebellion and "obey not the gospel of our Lord Jesus Christ". More than this we dare not say. Many Christians have believed that it involves everlasting conscious suffering. Some of our Lord's words seem to point to this, but possibly not conclusively. Hell is in eternity, which is not simply unending time, but a state beyond human ken. And if in God we live and move and have our being, it is hard to see how a human personality can continue even to suffer as a personality when finally banished from His presence. Of one thing we may be sure: hell is very terrible, and God has paid the price of Calvary to save us from it. "How shall we escape, if we neglect so great salvation?" (Heb. ii, 3).

The judgment is on the basis of works. This does not contradict the clear statements of Scripture that no-one is justified by his works. The things we do, as St. James reminds us, are the only demonstration we can give to others that we have received a new life from God. They are public evidences of our private standing before God. Therefore, since judgment is essentially a public matter, it will be these evidences which are appealed to to vindicate God's decisions. Man is condemned for his sins, not for his sinful nature. We are accepted by the grace of God, but our lives are required to bear testimony to the efficacy of that grace. Even then the final court of appeal is the Lamb's Book of Life—the roll of those who have received life through the sacrificial death of Christ. All others stand condemned, for no man's works can stand the scrutiny of God's holiness.

Judgment for the Christian is linked with reward in several passages (e.g. 1 Cor. iii, 13-15; 2 Cor. v, 10; Luke xix, 11-27). The identity of this "judgment-seat of Christ" with the "great white throne" of God's general judgment has been questioned by some, but it appears clearly that the use the Christian has made of his privileges here will determine his opportunities and usefulness in the service of heaven.

One last point. We began with God the Maker, and looked at something of the wonder of the material creation. This creation, we have seen, shared in the corruption brought about by sin: things have gone wrong, though God made them very good. The question arises whether the material creation will share also in the redemption and glory which is ours in Christ. Will man regain and exercise his forfeited position in relation to the animal world? We cannot say. There are hints as to something of the kind in Isa. xi, Rom. viii, 18-22, and similar passages. The apostle Peter calls Christ's coming the "times of restoration of all things" in Acts iii, 21, and Christ speaks of it as the re-creation or regeneration in Matt. xix, 28. But these are only hints, and we do well not to dogmatize about it. Some have looked for a time of earthly prosperity in which such passages as Isa. xi might be literally fulfilled during the mysterious "thousand years", but this cannot be directly proved from Scripture. In any event, the present creation is to pass away and we are to look for a new heaven and a new earth wherein dwelleth righteousness (Matt. xxiv, 35; Heb i, 11-12; 2 Pet. iii, 10-13; Rev. xxi, 1). Whether this world will have the same sort of continuity with the old one as our new bodies will have with our present ones we do not know. Once again we have stepped out of time into eternity, and it is not surprising that we find ourselves baffled.

What, then, of the glorious culmination of God's work of redemption in that state or place of destination which we usually call heaven? The word 'heaven' is in a sense misleading. The New Testament does not use this vague term in describing our eternal state. Heaven means simply the sky, and because man always thinks of God as above and around him, it is a natural, though anthropomorphic, term for the dwelling-place of God. God is everywhere, and the limitless expanse of heaven is an apt symbol of His presence. But there are dangers in its use; do we really want little children to think of their Friend as being "above the bright blue sky"? Is He not the Friend that sticketh closer than a brother?

Christ ascended after His Resurrection into the clouds; so it is natural for us to think of Him as there, especially since in this way He will also return. Therefore we think of our present spiritual possessions as reserved in heaven for us. But the Scripture speaks of our future home as the New Jerusalem—the spiritual counterpart of the earthly city of God—coming down out of heaven. It will be a community life centred in God Himself. We shall find there unlimited capacity and opportunity for praise and worship, for knowledge and service, for fellowship and holy pleasure (Rev. xxi-xxii, 8; 1 Cor. xiii, 8-10). Of course, all the description of precious stones and a golden street and harps is imagery—no human language can describe the presence of God—but it is something exceeding glorious, and man was made to enjoy it. This is the purpose for which God first created man—for fellowship with Himself. In this sphere alone man truly discovers himself; this is why our powers were given us, and we shall find our fullest freedom in the unremitting service of God. If it be true that "we lose ourselves in heaven above" . . . "lost in wonder, love and praise" . . . it is more true that we *find* ourselves there as nowhere else. Made like Christ, with His capacity for expression and for service, and able to know as fully as He now knows us, we enter on a life richer and fuller than we can ever imagine, and ourselves constitute an eternal example of the grace and power of God in creation, redemption, sanctification and glory.

SUMMARY OF SECTION III

Let us summarize the main steps of the plan according to which God is realizing in His universe the victory of Christ.

I. GOD IN ACTION

(1) *The Holy Trinity.* God is One in nature and will, but is revealed in Three Persons, Father, Son and Holy Spirit, each with His distinctive activity in the work of God as it relates to man.

(2) *The Holy Spirit.* The eternal Third Person of the Trinity is given to man in a new way at Pentecost and creates the Christian Church.

(3) *The Holy Scriptures.* The Bible is the unique authoritative revelation of God. It is the work of the Holy Spirit through the human authors, with the full collaboration of their personalities.

(4) *Sanctification.* The Spirit brings the Christian power for holy living, and seeks with his co-operation to transform him into the likeness of Christ, energizing his will and directing his desires. He demands yieldedness and renunciation of sin.

II. THE CHRISTIAN CHURCH

(1) *Membership.* The true Church consists of all those regenerated by the Spirit of God. The visible Church has always contained merely nominal members, and has had a chequered history: the true Church grows continually as others believe in Christ.

(2) *Mission.* The primary Mission of the Church is to preach the gospel and make disciples of all nations. She is also called to uphold moral standards, to do good to men, and to exhibit a pattern of community life.

(3) *Means of Grace.* God meets the needs of His people in many ways; notably in Prayer, Bible-Reading, Worship, through Preaching of the Gospel, and through the Sacraments of Baptism and Holy Communion.

III. The Consummation

(1) *The Second Coming.* The Church expects the Personal, Visible Return of Christ to establish openly the kingdom which is at present known only in the hearts of true Christians.

(2) *The Resurrection.* The dead, good and evil, will be raised in bodily form, not merely survive in spirit, and will stand before God as Judge.

(3) *Final Destiny.* The rebellious, and the rejecters of the gospel, are shut out for ever from the presence of God in Hell. Those whom God has redeemed enter a heaven of eternal glory.

We have traced in broad outline the development of God's plan from the creation to the consummation, from the beginning to the end of time. Many details have necessarily been excluded, many questions unanswered. Indeed, God has not satisfied all the questions of our curiosity, but He has told us all we need to know of His purpose. This purpose centres in Jesus Christ; by Him God made the worlds, through Him He has made redemption for sin, and in Him all will finally be summed up (Heb. i, 2; Eph. i, 10; Rom. xi, 36). His kingdom, unseen now except in the hearts of His people, will be openly set up when He returns, and the kingdom of this world becomes the kingdom of our God and of His Christ (Rev. xi, 15). Some will own Him King with the loyal devotion of their lives, and will rejoice to see Him publicly enthroned; others will bow to His Majesty because they have no alternative, their proud rebellion still unbroken. The issue is critical and divisive, but God will gather out all things that offend (Matt. xiii, 41); and finally the Son, His work completed, will hand over the kingdom to His Father, that God may be all in all (1 Cor. xv, 24-28).

EPILOGUE

CHRISTIANITY is not merely a body of teaching which demands our intellectual assent. Right thinking about God and the world is all-important, but it must lead to right living. It is a mistake to suppose that it does not matter what a man believes, so long as he lives a decent life, for his beliefs will greatly influence his estimate of himself and the direction of his exertions; further, such an argument leaves out of account entirely God's estimate of him as a whole man. But it is equally erroneous to imagine that if a man has right beliefs, his actions are of secondary importance. Christianity treats man as a whole and demands that his whole personality, thoughts, desires, will and deed shall be right in the sight of God. Christian doctrine can never be studied *in vacuo;* it challenges us on the plane of daily living. It tells me in the most uncompromising terms that I am a miserable sinner, and points me to Christ as the only means of deliverance. If I wholeheartedly assent to this, I have accepted a moral imperative. If I refuse to act, I have only myself to blame for the consequences; but the Christian experience has by the grace of God been put within my reach.

It should have been plain to the careful reader that Christians are not made by the acceptance of creeds, nor yet by moral effort to achieve a Christian standard of ethics. In fact, many Christians have a very poor intellectual grasp of the principles of their faith, and all would confess their shameful failure to attain the moral levels of the Sermon on the Mount. These things are the goals we set before us, not the gateway to the road. God has put the gateway within the reach of all; it is the experience which we have described as conversion. But to know about it is not the same as to experience it; that involves a personal interview with the risen Christ. Have you who read these words had faith to believe that He is alive today to help you? And have you assented to His condemnation of your sin and welcomed Him as your only Saviour, committing your case into His hands?

"To as many as received Him, to them gave He the right to become children of God, even to them that believe on His Name" (John i, 12, R.V.).

"If ye know these things, happy are ye if ye do them" (John xiii, 17).

APPENDICES

1. THE THEORY OF EVOLUTION

THE bitterest opposition to the Christian doctrine of creation comes from a certain class of scientist who believes that the problem is resolved by the single word 'Evolution'. It is easy to forget that unless the exact content of a word is expounded, and proves to be an adequate cause for the phenomena it is intended to explain, the mere giving of a name conveys nothing more than an excuse for ceasing to think. The confusion is increased by the fact that the word Evolution is used to mean two different things: (i) the Theory of Organic Evolution as a means whereby the present multiplicity of species of plants and animals originated; and (ii) a Philosophy of Progress which assumes that the process described by (i) is automatic, mechanistic, and applicable to man in the moral, intellectual and spiritual worlds, not only in the past but in the present and future.

The Theory of Organic Evolution was put forward by Charles Darwin in his book, *The Origin of Species*. It postulates that the various forms of life have originated from a common ancestor in the ordinary processes of reproduction: i.e. it is a doctrine of "derivation by descent". Darwin still believed that God created life in the first place. The fact that the mechanism of the process suggested by Darwin has been regarded as unlikely does not mean that biologists have abandoned the doctrine itself.

The doctrine denoted by (ii) is obtained by analogy and extension of the theory we have called (i). It can hardly be said to be based on scientific evidence as such; what evidence there is about man would hardly lead us to suppose he is advancing spiritually! It is an act of faith on the part of the materialist as much as the Christian's view is on his part. In fact, it might even be said to tax credulity further, and to bear out the words of the apostle concerning the pagan world "they did not like to have God in their knowledge"

(Rom. i, 28, R.V.). It is clear that Christianity, with its doctrine of the fall and its outlook on history, is totally opposed to this human philosophy which flatters man and makes his dependence on God unnecessary. Unfortunately, it is often taught, in popular literature and to the young, as if it were an automatic consequence of (i). The average man's thinking has become permeated with it.

With regard to (i), the Theory of Evolution proper, Christians might do well to reserve their judgment. It is a matter for collection and interpretation of scientific evidence, though Christians have often suspected, probably not unjustifiably, that the evidence has not always been fairly handled because of the investigator's leanings towards the philosophy of automatic progress. Only a few remarks on this subject can here be made; a further treatment must be looked for elsewhere. [1]

To begin with, it is often glibly and categorically stated that the Church has been the champion of reaction and the opponent of scientific progress all down her history. We must beware of such statements: they rest on ambiguities. If by the Church is meant the medieval unreformed Roman Church we may admit some truth in the charge, though the opposition has been exaggerated greatly. But if we mean the body of Christians generally, we have only to point to devout and reverent Christians like Isaac Newton, Michael Faraday, Clerk Maxwell, to see how false it is. Christians have rightly opposed scientific claims to interpret the whole universe mechanistically on the sole basis of observational data: e.g. they have opposed the deduction of Evolution (ii) from Evolution (i). Some have with rather misguided zeal invaded scientific territory and passed judgment on the scientific evidence itself. This may at times have been justified, but it has provoked a not surprising hostility. It is wiser to face the evidence fairly.

There is a considerable body of evidence which suggests that to a limited extent evolution by fairly continuous change

[1] E.g. in *Modern Discovery and the Bible*, Prof. Rendle Short (I.V.F.), Chapters I-V.

has taken place and, indeed, is still doing so. For example, it is quite reasonable to suppose that the whole cat tribe, from the lion to the domestic pussy, may have developed by continuous modification from a few original pairs. But it is quite another matter when it comes to widening the range of evolution, and gaps as yet unbridgeable remain, notably between living and non-living, plant and animal, beast and man. Evidence of this kind of change is of the scantiest and its interpretation highly precarious. It is in many cases almost impossible to conceive how intermediate types could have had any stable existence for periods long enough for the development to have taken place.

The writer's own view, for what it is worth, is that evolution of a continuous character has been very limited, and that God has moved by stages of rapid organized change—perhaps by special creation of new types, perhaps by special modification of existing types to fit into a new environment. But either way, there is nothing mechanical or automatic about it. The Christian must firmly hold that whether God created by instantaneous act, by a succession of steps, or by continuous change, it was *God's* directive will behind it all.

He has two strong arguments on his side. The first is the argument from Balance. Nature is very delicately poised. Man has learnt this to his cost. A few rabbits accidentally introduced into Australia became a continent-wide plague in a few years. A striking example on a small scale is given by Dr. Osborne Greenwood.[1]

A certain Mediterranean plant called the Yucca opens its flowers for one night only. If fertilized, each flower produces two hundred ovules. One insect only can effect fertilization, the Yucca moth (*Pronuba*). This it does by kneading the pollen into a ball and carrying it to the stigma of another flower. It exacts toll from the Yucca by piercing the stigma with its ovipositor and laying four eggs, no more and no less, in the ovary of each flower. Each developing larva eats twenty-five seeds, thus leaving the Yucca 50 per cent for propagation.

[1] In *Christianity and the Mechanists*, by H. W. Osborne Greenwood, M.D., F.R.S.E. (Religious Book Club).

The arrangement is thus to the benefit of both partners, but a slight modification of the proportions would result in both moth and flower being stamped out. There are far too many such cases to be accounted for by saying that all the unsuccessful attempts perished. Also it is hard to conceive how such an arrangement could arise gradually without some directive Mind to control it. Or are we to imagine that *Pronuba* can count?

The same example provides an illustration for the other argument, which is that from Instinct. A half-formed instinct is of no use to anyone. Indeed, it may be a danger to the species. A spider spins a web by a long chain of processes which are unchanging and mechanical. They have been thought to be 'inherited experience', though this view presents many difficulties. But of what use were the half-formed webs of the countless generations of spiders who learnt the process bit by bit? Without the final viscous spiral the web is useless to the spider. What Mind directed the chain of operations? Certainly not the spider's.

Finally, we ought perhaps to say a word about the record in Genesis i. We have given reasons in Chapter VII for regarding this as authoritative. Science confirms in detail the order of creation there depicted. But acceptance of Genesis i does not compel us to imagine that God's acts were always instantaneous, or that when He is said to create or make (the difference may be significant) it is always implied that He created *ex nihilo*. This is certainly true of the initial creation of the material universe, but subsequently He may merely have moulded existing material. We are distinctly told that Adam's body was made in this way (Gen. ii, 7). Regarded in this way, there is no real antithesis between the record and scientific evidence.

The Christian must tenaciously hold that God made and maintains His world; he may have full confidence in the scriptural record attested by his Master;[1] but he will do well to leave the 'how' to the experts, unless, of course, it happens to be his own chosen field of specialized study and investigation.

[1] *See* e.g. in Matt. xix, 4; Mark xiii, 19; John v, 46-47.

II. MIRACLES IN THE OLD TESTAMENT

DIFFICULTIES sometimes arise for the modern mind in connection with the miraculous element in the Old Testament record. Miracles in the New Testament are either performed by Christ Himself, or by His disciples, in the early stages of the Church's witness, when filled with the power of the Holy Spirit. They seem, perhaps, more in keeping with the tremendous character of the events they accompany than the Old Testament miracles appear to do. There is only room here for a few remarks; for fuller treatment the reader is referred to such works as Canon T. C. Hammond's *In Understanding Be Men*, Fourth Edition, p. 68, *The New Bible Handbook* (I.V.F.), pp. 56 ff., or *Is the Bible True?* by Dr. B. F. C. Atkinson, Chapter V.

Natural law is, as we have tried to show, a demonstration of God's power. The fact that certain 'laws' of this kind are discoverable by man is due to the orderliness and consistency of the character of God. God works to a plan, and the behaviour of the world is to a large extent determined and predictable. Reasonable life and intercourse would be impossible if it were otherwise. We have seen also that God controls human history, but in the same way His control is usually by means of, rather than in spite of, the natural development of human character, and the law by which man reaps what he has sown. But that does not mean we can rule the miraculous out of court altogether. God can certainly override His own laws, just as man can set aside the blind forces of inanimate matter. If I let go of a knife it will fall, but I could equally well throw it up to stick in the ceiling. I am not defying gravity, but overruling it by a higher power in my muscles. Such events must, however, be rare if the world is to have a consistent meaning. So also an alarm-clock has a double mechanism: a regular ticking for time-keeping, and the sudden alarm for special occasions. An alarm-clock which rang the bell every half-hour would be a useless frivolity. God is not frivolous, and does not so act without due cause.

Many 'miracles' are due rather to 'natural' events happening at the right time than to supernatural interference. The earthquake which seems to have caused the fall of the walls of Jericho (Joshua vi, 20),[1] the landslide which may have dammed the Jordan (Joshua iii, 16),[2] and the wind which dried up the Red Sea (Exod. xiv, 21) appear to be of this type.

Other occasions where God modified His laws in a miraculous act seem to have occurred mainly in three great periods: at the exodus from Egypt when God was forging Israel into a nation and binding them by covenant to Him; the days of Elijah and Elisha when He was recalling the idolatrous people to faith in Him as their all-sufficient Lord; and the days of our Lord and the beginning of the Church. In each case we may see adequate spiritual reason for the supernatural events if we approach the matter humbly and with insight into God's purposes. How much poorer would be our knowledge of God's ways if Naaman had never been recovered of his leprosy, and the widow's cruse of oil had not been multiplied.

We must not forget that always the greatest miracles are the spiritual ones. God can check and change the course of a man's character and behaviour by the power of His Spirit in the New Birth, as we have shown in Chapters VI and VII. This has an effect on the course of human history which is infinitely greater than miracles, say, of healing or feeding the body. As our Lord once said: "Whether is easier, to say, Thy sins are forgiven thee; or to say, Arise and walk?" (Luke v, 23, R.V.).

III. THE TERMINOLOGY OF ATONEMENT

In Chapter V we have avoided as far as possible the use of 'technical' language in describing the work of our Lord on the Cross. Certain words, however, are frequently used and occur in our English Bibles, so that an explanation is called for.

[1] Cf. Rendle Short, *Modern Discovery and the Bible*, p. 153f., and refs.
[2] Ibid.

Atonement is used nowadays in most cases to mean the whole doctrine of the Cross. In our English Old Testament it means "covering of sin", and is explained in Rom. iii, 25-26, where God is said to justify His action in forgiving Israel's sins by the sacrifice of Christ. The blood of bulls and goats did not *take away* sin, though God forgave the sin of the faithful offerer. The sin was covered, to be taken away in Christ. In the New Testament (A.V.) the word occurs only once (Rom. v, 11), where it would more rightly be translated 'reconciliation' (see R.V.), the old root-meaning of the English word.

Reconciliation emphasizes the results of Christ's work in restoring our relationship with God—we may now be at one with Him, our guilt being removed.

Redemption emphasizes the cost to our Saviour of our deliverance by which we are released from Satan's power and belong to Christ. "Ye are not your own, ye are bought with a price," says St. Paul (1 Cor. vi, 19-20), and St. Peter means the same when he describes us as "redeemed with the precious blood of Christ" (1 Pet. i, 18-19). Some earlier Christians believed that the price was paid to Satan, but the word need not imply any recipient.

Propitiation is used to describe our Lord in Rom. iii, 25, 1 John ii, 2, and iv, 10. It is the word used for the mercy-seat in the Tabernacle in the Septuagint Greek Version of the Old Testament, and it means that Christ's death was a place where God and man might meet and favour could be shown again from God to man. It should be clear that it does not mean that God was there *made* favourable to man: God's grace provided the Sacrifice as a way by which man might approach Him without being exposed to His holy wrath against sin.

For a full discussion of these points and of the whole doctrine of the Atonement the reader is referred to *The Death of Christ*, by James Denney, and to *Why the Cross?* by the late Archdeacon H. E. Guillebaud, both published by the I.V.F.

IV. BIBLE DIFFICULTIES

THIS is a vast subject, and for a full treatment the reader must be referred to other books, notably *Some Moral Difficulties of the Bible*, by the late Archdeacon H. E. Guillebaud and others, and *Modern Discovery and the Bible*, by the late Prof. A. Rendle Short, both published by the I.V.F. Only a few lines can be added here.

The reader may perhaps feel that the position outlined in Chapter VII with regard to the Bible is too uncompromising in the light of modern thought and is not borne out by the facts. It is, however, the firm conviction of the writer that the Bible can resist all attacks made upon it. These have come along three main lines:

(*a*) Supposed moral inconsistencies, especially between the early Old Testament and the teaching of Christ. These are discussed in the first book mentioned above. Suffice it to say here that the writer holds it to be possible to believe in a revelation which is progressive, but none the less a revelation and not a groping after God. We do not teach the Calculus to eight-year-olds, but the fact that they know only the whole numbers does not mean their arithmetic is wrong, even if they do say "2 into 7 you can't!"

(*b*) Supposed errors in historical facts, and internal discrepancies between parallel accounts. Many of these disappear on investigation. Some numerical errors are obviously due to faults in the long transmission of the documents down to the present day. Numerals are easy to miscopy, and the earliest Old Testament MS. extant is at least 1,000 years later than its date of composition. In any case, the Bible is an ancient document, so why, when it disagrees with other historical documents often less ancient, should it always be the Bible that is wrong?

(*c*) Supposed errors in scientific facts. Some of these have been discussed earlier, and Prof. Rendle Short's book gives a detailed investigation. The Bible uses the language of phenomena, describing events as man sees them. It is not a scientific text-book, but it is often remarkably accurate. God hangs the earth on nothing, says Job (xxvi, 7), but a contemporary civilization, the Hindu, believed that it rested on the backs of six elephants!

SUGGESTIONS FOR FURTHER READING

This is not an exhaustive Bibliography, nor are all the books in agreement with the method of treatment adopted in the previous chapters. They are simply books that may be of help to those who want to read more deeply. The more popular books are given at the beginning of each section; works of reference at the end.

GENERAL

What the Church Teaches, Bishop Blunt (Penguin).
The Catholic Faith, W. H. Griffith Thomas (Longmans).
In Understanding Be Men, T. C. Hammond (Inter-Varsity Fellowship).
The Christian Faith in the Modern World, J. G. Machen (Macmillan).
Outlines of Theology, A. A. Hodge (Eerdmans).
Principles of Theology, W. H. Griffith Thomas (Longmans).
The Infallible Word, N. B. Stonehouse and P. Woolley (Tyndale Press).

GOD AND CREATION

Modern Discovery and the Bible, A. Rendle Short (Inter-Varsity Fellowship).
The Universe and God, R. E. D. Clark (Hodder & Stoughton).
The Christian Apprehension of God, H. R. Mackintosh (Nisbet).
The Christian View of God and the World, James Orr (Elliott).

MAN AND SIN

The Holy War, John Bunyan (R.T.S.).
The Problem of Pain, C. S. Lewis (Geoffrey Bles).
The Plight of Man and the Power of God, D. M. Lloyd-Jones (Pickering & Inglis).
Some Moral Difficulties of the Bible, H. E. Guillebaud (Inter-Varsity Fellowship).

JESUS CHRIST

The Life of Jesus Christ, James Stalker (T. & T. Clark).

The Fact of Christ, P. Carnegie Simpson (Hodder & Stoughton).

Why the Cross? H. E. Guillebaud (Inter-Varsity Fellowship).

Who Moved the Stone? Frank Morison (Faber & Faber).

The Virgin Birth of Christ, J. G. Machen (Marshall Morgan & Scott).

The Atonement, R. W. Dale (Independent Press).

THE HOLY SPIRIT AND THE CHURCH

Christian Behaviour, C. S. Lewis (Geoffrey Bles).

Valiant in Fight, B. F. C. Atkinson (Inter-Varsity Fellowship).

The Spirit of God, G. Campbell Morgan (Marshall Morgan & Scott).

The Holy Spirit of God, W. H. Griffith Thomas (Longmans).

He that is Spiritual, L. Sperry-Chafer (Marshall Morgan & Scott).

The Promise of His Coming, C. F. Hogg & J. B. Watson (Pickering & Inglis).

Ecce Venit, A. J. Gordon (Hodder & Stoughton).

INDEX